Dear Gabriel

Letters from a Trainee Angel

Joanna Infeld

Cover painting by Karina Edwards

ISBN 13: 978-0-9760512-8-2
ISBN 10: 0-9760512-8-1

Printed in the United States of America

KO
RA

**KORA
PRESS**

From the author

Why do I believe in angels? Simply because I have found places in the world where something angelic, or an entity or an essence, lives in the land. The reason that I know of its existence is that when I connect to it, it always floods me with great wellbeing which is accompanied by two predominant feelings, no matter what I am doing or thinking about when this happens: the first is a profound awe at the beauty of the planet, which seems to permeate every cell in my body, and the second is a deep feeling of being grateful for being alive and not wanting to waste even one moment of this short, meaningful existence. The reason I know that this presence is domiciled in the land is because I cannot connect to these feelings and sensations in the same way anywhere else, even though I have tried. Yes, I have memories of them and I can think along the lines that they have introduced me to, but it is not the same; it is never such a throughout and total experience.

I have decided to let one of these angels speak through me and it has caused me to write down the thoughts and stories included in this book. I wanted there to be a plot, perhaps a love story, perhaps some thrilling adventures that would ensure that the book would sell. The angel would have nothing of the kind and so it told its own story. I am only the transmitter, the recorder, the "post office."

This is not channeling, as I understand channeling to be, for I stand against the idea of handing over one's consciousness and thus offering up control of one's senses and discernment to an unknown intelligence, whether through hypnosis or trance or any other means, with the one exception of sleep which is both natural and necessary to one's continuance and wellbeing.

Thus, this is a record of the struggle of a trainee angel, sent to planet Earth to help the human race at this vital time in human history. There is not a lot one little angel can do, and yet, as the human race becomes more sensitive and receptive (and I believe this is indeed happening), perhaps we will learn to listen and respond to those higher universal intelligences and entities that are continuously trying to avert our attention from the lure of the material worlds towards the rules of the spiritual realms that await us.

Week one

Dear Gabriel

Thank you for choosing me for the privilege and honor to be sent to Earth to assist the human beings who live here, so that they may become more ready for the changes that are soon to unfold on the beautiful blue planet of theirs. I feel that I have a lot to learn and that this tasking will be a challenge and an opportunity both at the same time. I will do my best and I hope that I may become a fully-fledged angel as a result of this undertaking.

I understand that I am to stay here for an earthly year, or one revolution of this planet around their sun. I will be reporting to you every seven days (days being rotations around the Earth's axis).

I have heard a lot about humans during my time at the Angel Academy and I realize that they are a stubborn lot and not easily persuaded, even if the persuasion is in their favor and for their own good. As requested, I will be reporting regularly to you with my impressions and concerns and I do hope you can be proud of my efforts.

Determined to earn my wings,

Hark
the trainee angel

Week two

Dear Gabriel

I am writing this letter to you after merely seven Earth days since I was dropped off on this blue planet, having been briefed about my duties here. It is not at all as I had expected. I find it so difficult to get my bearings and to know how best to proceed. Everything moves so fast and no one has stopped to listen to me yet. Getting used to the pace of everyday life here is the hardest thing for me to accomplish at the moment. I am used to the serenity of our angelic dealings, to the harmony of the spheres and to an equilibrium of sensations. But here on Earth everything is so different, full of disturbance, discord and mostly unnecessary haste.

People here talk a lot about angels and they say they believe in us; they even have stories, books, videos, jewelry and other paraphernalia named after us, but when we try to help them, they completely ignore us and move in a different direction. They are seldom still enough for long enough to listen to anything from the unseen worlds trying to communicate to them and when they do stop the incessant activity of theirs for a moment, they are usually so tired from rushing around all day that they are hardly in a place to listen to anything except their own brains whirring around, producing more worry and anxiety for them to occupy themselves with.

I don't know how to get their attention and so far I am failing miserably in trying to turn their minds and faculties towards God, creation and the harmony that exists within the universe, the natural worlds of planet Earth and within their own bodies.

Please advise how to proceed so that I may become an angel worthy of the title.

In anticipation,

Hark

the trainee angel

Week three

Dear Gabriel

Another period of time has passed since last I wrote to you, time measured on Earth in what are called days, weeks, months and years. One week consists of seven days or seven rotations of the Earth around its planetary axis. Months are unequally divided into 28, 30 or 31 days (except for what is called leap year, when one month—February—has 29 days to compensate for the fact that it takes close to 365 and a quarter days for the Earth to circumnavigate the sun).

I feel a little bit more settled now and I am learning to speed up so that I might capture a moment in some human's busy thought processes to make a slender connection, which tends to last for a few seconds only. But I did manage, about five rotations ago, to connect to a young human who has been on this planet for the duration of ten revolutions around the sun, which humans here call years. This child was out in the garden playing and suddenly, in the middle of his running around, chasing his dog (which is a domesticated animal humans call a pet), he thought and pondered for a moment, "Why am I here? Why me? What is it all about?" At that moment I was with him. I do know and remember that we are not allowed to influence the thoughts of humans, but I was there in encouragement and support.

The moment did not last, but it gave me hope that perhaps I can be of use on planet Earth after all, if I can only find the right person at the right time to communicate to. It seems that children are more likely candidates, so I will from now on pay more attention to the younger generation and their thought processes. Perhaps that way I can be of better support and service to the adults of tomorrow, who are the children of today.

In hope,

Hark

the trainee angel

Week four

Dear Gabriel

As more time passes here on planet Earth, I find this to be a very strange place indeed. It has taken me time to get used to the concept of time according to which the evolutions and rotations of planets are measured here. These understandings appear to be very important to humans, to the point where their preoccupation with the number of revolutions around the sun they have witnessed in their lifetime becomes of paramount significance. They are forever asking each other and declaring to others of their species how many cycles of seasons they have attended since birth. Then, after a certain age, they stop talking about it but continue to guess each other's longevity. They seem to think, for some strange, unknown by me as yet reason, that it is better to have gone through fewer planetary revolutions rather than more and they spend much time and effort in concealing their age and being able to appear younger than their years would indicate.

There seems to be a prevalent fear of growing old, for the wisdom and experience of old age on the whole is not respected or attended to. Unlike our understanding that longevity means seniority, experience, knowledge and wisdom, to the human it mostly means isolation, disease and fear of loneliness and dying. I think that if humans realized the potential of the life they can have after the one they are so attached to here on Earth, they might be able to let go a little bit more easily. And if there was more value for the wisdom of experience, perhaps people would see the importance of offering the old folks security and a place within their society, rather than isolating them from it.

I understand that there was a time in human history when old age signified wisdom and death meant release from planetary duty and neither were feared or avoided, but anticipated and prepared for. There was a time when those with greater experience would offer advice and learning to the young who were honored to be able to offer care and support in return. However, these times are now relegated to history and myth, and old age and death are both handled by so-called experts, mostly away from society and the fearful gaze of others who know they are unavoidably heading the same way, too.

This is only one of the many confusing aspects I have encountered on my earthly journey so far. In trying to better understand the humans I hope to communicate with I have been attempting to unravel the meaning of this game humans play (I do see concealing one's age and guessing the age of others as a game). I do wonder what they would think of the mature age of, for example, an archangel, running into several thousands of revolutions of their planet around the sun, or a young angel, like myself, who is barely a few hundred years old.

In discovery mode,

Hark

the trainee angel

Week five

Dear Gabriel

There is another game people play—they like to use words to describe something that mean something else. This can become very confusing, but it has been an interesting challenge to try and understand *human-speak*. For example, they call their children kids, whereas the word kid is a label to describe a young goat. They also use various names to refer to each other, supposedly with endearment, but I am finding these euphemisms confusing. A man might refer to his girlfriend as a baby and a woman also might call her husband or her boyfriend baby. But they don't call their babies baby. No, their babies are their angels, honeys, sweeties, pumpkins, buddies or sugars (usually something sweet).

If you listen to their songs, they are full of babies—I have never heard so many entreaties, vows, declarations of everlasting love as in the lyrics to those musical statements of theirs.

Then there are the many animal epithets that they use to describe human qualities. So, for example, a pig is someone who is dirty or nasty or vulgar; a fox is someone who is sly and cannot be trusted; a bear is usually a name used to refer to a large man who is soft and gentle inside; a swine is someone who acts to the detriment of others; a puppy is a young person who lacks experience; a monkey is a mischievous, playful and cheeky person ("you cheeky monkey" they say to each other with endearment); to rat is to tell-tale on someone; a mouse is someone who is quiet, taciturn and prefers to be inconspicuous; an ant is someone who works hard in a mechanical way and a workhorse is a person who takes on more than their fair share of effort; a dragon is usually a fierce woman and a parrot is someone who repeats what others have said, and to ape is to copy the actions of another. An ox is someone who is strong; a chicken is someone who is scared; a snake is someone who is two-faced and speaks with a forked tongue; a gazelle is a graceful woman; a wolf is a predator; sheep are mindless followers, a sloth is a lazy person, a magpie is someone who likes trinkets, baubles and other shiny objects used for decoration or display; a peacock is someone who likes to show off and cold turkey means to come off a habit, like drugs or alcohol abuse, by suddenly cutting oneself off without gradual build-up.

The list is endless and there are probably as many labels from the flora worlds—like strong as an oak tree, cool as a cucumber or fresh as a daisy. Comparison is a favorite pastime of these curious creatures; people, places and situations are forever reminding them of other people, places and situations. Nothing is of itself, and yet they do not understand that all is connected and all is one.

Looking for the obvious,

Hark
the trainee angel

Week six

Dear Gabriel

It is quite curious how humans love to classify things and box them and label them. I think it makes them feel like they are in control—they do love to manage everything. Take, for example, the marvelous phenomenon of day and night which, as you know, is an alternating occurrence here on Earth. In order to calculate and organize this continuous stream of alterations and alternations, humans have instituted what they call a calendar. There have been many attempts to thus divide a year into segments, a year being a natural division of one revolution of this planet around their sun. However, in these modern times most humans have agreed to follow and abide by a single calendar which divides days into weeks and months. Weeks are units consisting of seven days and this division influences everything that humans do and how they plan for the future. It means that they repeat many activities in seven day intervals, as they undertake to fulfill various taskings on specific days. People who adhere to the many diverse religions here set aside one day a week as a holy day, during which they worship their God and pray, but they cannot agree which day it is supposed to be, so, depending on their religion it is either a Friday (Islam), Saturday (Judaism) or Sunday (Christianity).

Mostly humans do not work during their holy days, though this is changing as they seem to need to work more and more to earn more, sell more and make more. It is almost as though the whole world is speeding up with more to do, to make, to have.

The Babylonians were the ones who had registered, noted and established the correlation between the days of the week and the influence of the various planets, the sun and the moon on Earth during the seven days of the week. This is reflected in some languages, particularly in French and to some degree in English, with Monday being the day of the moon, Saturday the day of Saturn and Sunday the day of the sun. The French language also reflects the fact that the influence of Mercury is strongest on Wednesday, the influence of Mars the strongest on Tuesday and the influence of Venus the strongest on Friday. That leaves Thursday, which is dedicated to the frequency of Jupiter or Thor, the equivalent Norse god.

So, as humans are so dependent on this sequence of planetary influences, they have an urgent need for calendars and diaries; as a result they tend to do things on a repetitive basis, mostly weekly or every seven days. So, for example, if a young human is studying for a degree, then he or she will have different classes on a Monday, a Tuesday, a Wednesday and so on. Even their leisure activities are often repeated on a weekly basis; so for example, there might be baseball practice on a Saturday or ballet on a Wednesday afternoon and so on. This does not allow for much spontaneity and I am worried that humans are losing their ability to respond to the changing frequencies that come to them from creation and keep changing on a daily, weekly and minute by minute basis. So some days might be more conducive to a certain activity or the atmosphere might be just right to, for example, play music, but the human is so busy trying to fulfill his or her schedule that he or she will no doubt miss this opportunity and never connect to the inspiration that would have been there for them if they were to respond to their own intuition and feeling, which is always speaking to them, but they mostly are too busy to listen.

Bewildered,

Hark

the trainee angel

Week seven

Dear Gabriel

It has been quite difficult to find the times when humans are open to receive messages from an angel or any other higher entity that might be attempting to communicate with them that day. At first I thought it would be during their holy days when they are a little bit more relaxed and have set time aside to devote to their religion. However, I found this not necessarily to be so, because mostly their religion is planned and organized according to a schedule that has already been filled and pre-decided.

Through trial and error I can now say that I have successfully discovered their most relaxed and open times when I can attempt to pass on a message, a thought or a subject for contemplation. It is during their evening ablution times, when they are getting ready to go to bed and are winding down after a busy day—that is when their guards are lowered and they are open to think of something new. Providing, of course, that they are not bothered by something that had happened during the day, or angered, upset or otherwise emotionally disturbed (which unfortunately does happen often).

The best time of all and the easiest for a small angel to get past their defences—their shields and armory— is during a shower, for when they stand under running water, the water cleans their aura and takes away their stresses, worries and other tensions that tend to stiffen their muscles, especially around their necks and shoulders. Many jobs and occupations today require hours of sitting at a computer, a phone, a desk or a till, and these persistent unnatural postures of theirs add to their muscle fatigue and strain.

So I have been waiting for these occasions when the shower is turned on and the weary human steps under the flow of water—this is my time, for as the stresses leave the body, so higher energy food can come in.

One other time that is good for communicating to these humans on planet Earth is when they are physically emptying out, otherwise known as sitting on the toilet. This too is a good time to sneak past their defences and send them useful messages. (I think humans would be horrified to hear me saying this, but they do enjoy the little inspirations they receive at these private times.)

The third time I have found effective in this pursuit of mine is the time just before sleep when the human is feeling relaxed, drowsy and is heading into unconsciousness. The only problem with this time of day is that mostly they will then fall asleep and even if the message has been received, it will not be remembered by morning. Some people do keep a pad of paper and a pen by their bedside because they know this is a time of new ideas and inspirations, but these are the diligent few rather than the many.

If all else fails and there is an urgent message to impart, say from a deceased loved one, a guardian or a teacher (and they all have these special beings who look after them day and night, otherwise they could never survive another day), I do so when they are asleep, manufacturing dreams that are meaningful, conveying messages that will hopefully jog their memory and influence their actions and thoughts. The rest is up to the individual.

Here too, though, the problem is getting them to remember and then heeding the advice. Sometimes they will remember in the morning but by lunchtime my carefully configured dream tableau will most often have been dismissed or otherwise forgotten.

Trying to connect,

Hark
the trainee angel

Week eight

Dear Gabriel

Oh joy! My first task on Earth has been accomplished! Although it was the smallest on my list of charges, there were moments when I was afraid that it would never happen. And then suddenly, I did it. Or rather, and I must remember not to claim credit for something that happened outside of myself—it happened and I was at the right place at the right time to observe it happening.

If you remember my list of tasks, the writing of which you yourself, oh Illumined One, had supervised, it includes one simple duty: find an earthly human who turns their mind and faculty to God, the Almighty One, not in search of personal gain, not to demonstrate to others their religious devotion, not with a request to be bailed out of trouble or a difficult situation, not in an emergency, not out of pride or greed, not in doubt or in pain, not in sickness or in suffering and certainly not when faced with danger, despair or death.

So there I was, still in observation mode, trying to find out more about these strange bipeds called humans. (And I must tell you on another occasion about the very humorous way in which they see ourselves, for they think we look like them, only apart from two arms, two legs and a head, they depict us with two wings to help us fly. I guess they cannot imagine that anything without wings could move around in the air; even their flying machines have wings! Some of their so-called artwork shows us as looking like their human children, with fat faces, naked bodies, and, of course, the obligatory wings!)

I was watching the behavior of the young, to try and find out where their very strange ways of thinking originate from and trying to detect when the formation of their character begins, when I saw a young child of perhaps five or six revolutions around their yellow star (which they call the sun) playing in the garden with his toys. His earthly mother had called him in to get ready for bed. It was after supper and the sun was setting and a cool breeze was beginning to blow in from the north. His mother had called him in several times before and on each occasion he had asked for an extension of his time with his playthings and his pet cat (as I mentioned before, a pet is the name humans give to other planetary creatures when they adopt them for companionship or protection, rather than commercial gain or scientific experiments). Finally the boy, in response to the insistent voice of his mother (and he knew well how far he could push it to get his own way), ran into the house, undressed, washed quickly and jumped into bed. His mother came into his room to tuck him in and say goodnight, and she asked the usual questions:

"Did you wash well?"

"Yes."

"Did your brush your teeth?"

"Yes."

"Did you say your prayers?"

"Must I?"

"Yes, you must. Go on, do it."

So he jumped out of bed, knelt down and said in a

very hurried voice: "Thank you God for the day and my toys and the garden and Spotty my cat. Thank you for looking after me, my mommy and my daddy and all my friends. Thank you God, Amen."

And back into bed he jumped, already almost asleep.

"Good night," he said as he snuggled up and as Spotty jumped onto the bed and curled up in her usual spot at his feet.

"Good night," said his mother as she kissed him good night and turned off the light.

Thus, this tasking now completed, I will turn my attention to further duties.

With satisfaction,

Hark

the trainee angel

Week nine

Dear Gabriel

Humans are so strange. I just can't get used to their funny and ridiculous ways. They do have eyes and ears and brains and yet it would seem that they can neither see nor hear nor think. It is almost as if mostly they inhabit a body but do not know how to use it properly and thus they are satisfied with using about three percent of their potential, exclaiming as they do so, "Isn't life fantastic?" and believing that they know what they are talking about.

One aspect I find especially frustrating in trying to fulfill the many tasks I have been given is to do with the fact that humans don't seem to learn from their mistakes. It would appear that each generation has to start all over again and that as a race their history does not appear to teach them anything new. The strangest thing is that they do learn history at school but this does not seem to make any difference at all. For example, you would think that in a world that has had several natural catastrophes inflicted upon it, such as floods, ice ages, earthquakes and volcanic eruptions, and has suffered many other disasters such as various epidemics that have intermittently decimated the populations of the world, people would have learned to expect the unexpected and to know that inevitably another great change is coming. In fact there is no nation and no country in the world that has not experienced war and great upheaval in the past, though some more so than others and some more recently than others. Then there are the many revolutions, large and small, uprisings, coups, religious revivals, rebellions, separatist movements, ethnic cleansings, genocide, territorial expansionism, imperialism, dominance, tyranny, slavery, colonialism and all forms of human self-inflicted misery, persecution, torture and exploitation. Why do people always think it will not happen to them and that life will simply continue in the same old ways, when they know that the human is destroying natural ecologies and habitats one by one, that the weather patterns are changing and that even the rays of the life giving star they call their sun are becoming deadly to them in too much concentrate and unsafe to be in for too long, due to the pollution of the atmosphere and the destruction of their protective ozone layer?

Can't they see change coming? All the great prophets have warned them of these changing times and many other clairvoyant and wise individuals have told them to take notice of the trends of history, and yet somehow they think it will not happen to them. It makes me think about a story I overheard of a Jewish couple who lived in Bucharest during the Second World War—when offered a place on the last boat leaving for Palestine before the Nazi invasion of Rumania, despite the fact of being shown clippings of newspapers describing Nazi atrocities against the Jews in Budapest, they decided to stay put because their new furniture was being delivered in a week's time. It seems that the world is still waiting for its furniture to be delivered and is insisting that nothing untoward can happen to it and that water will always be water and some guardian angel will protect them. But I don't see how a whole host of angels can protect anybody if they don't even protect the planet they live on and the ecology that supports them!

In exasperation,

Hark
the trainee angel

Week ten

Dear Gabriel

There is a new generation appearing here on planet Earth. They are called indigo children, though many of them are no longer children and are growing up fast. The reason they are called indigo is that during their birth an indigo glow or radiation was seen around them. These people have unusual abilities and skills—they are often clairvoyant, they have healing and telepathic abilities. It is no coincidence that these children are appearing at this time, when the world needs global change and a new type of leader.

I remember how you explained to us at the Angel Academy that the human children being born at this time have the oldest, most advanced genetic, a genetic that has had the longest time to evolve and refine. Thus the youngest child on planet Earth houses the oldest human genetic. And so these indigo children are carriers of a new genetic that will further evolve in the years to come. Already they are honing their skills and learning to live amongst people who don't necessarily understand them or believe what they are saying.

It is late in the day for this blue planet of theirs and Earth needs its champions—leaders that are selfless, concerned for the environment and guided by their understanding of the needs of the future. I feel very encouraged to see these young humans developing their sensitivity to the needs of the future and a desire to change the course of history. It is a race against time and time is running out.

I do believe that the human race will come to its senses (with a little bit of help) and take up the stewardship of this planet of theirs, rather than continue to be motivated by possession, profit and greed.

Proud to be part of the solution,

Hark

the trainee angel

Week eleven

Dear Gabriel

Thank you for your message and for your permission to move to stage two of my journey here on Earth in order to fulfill some further taskings. I tried to communicate clairvoyantly yesterday with a young girl and I felt I was making some progress. Through her I began to appreciate the difficulty one encounters when trapped in a physical body—it makes one feel very strange and lethargic. Because of the limitations of a body, humans have to move through holes in walls they call doors, as they cannot pass through inanimate objects like we can. They are also confined to the element of earth and are not able to fly through the air, unless they do so in one of the flying machines of theirs, called airplanes or helicopters, which are very heavy, large and awkward and sometimes even fall out of the sky, killing all those trapped within. As far as moving from place to place by means of walking is concerned, it must be a very strange business having to continuously place one foot in front of the other.

Apart from that a body must feel very heavy indeed as it weighs anything from a few (the weight of a baby) to several hundred pounds. It must take a lot of effort for them to even lift an arm or leg or to move at any decent speed at all. It is a miracle that they do not bump into things all the time and bruise their bodies which, of course, are only on loan to them for a short time. Thank God (literally) for the design which heals itself and adjusts with ease to new situations, for these souls, once they grow up in a body and learn to move it and work it with ease, seem to think that it is the most natural mode of living there is and they try to stretch its endurance and maneuverability to its limits. They even tend to bring together all those who have mastered various ways of moving their bodies to find out who can run the quickest or jump the highest. And then, following the example of the ancient Greeks, every four revolutions around their sun, they line up all the winners of these competitions of theirs to discover who is best in the world and they reward them with pieces of metal to honor their feats of endurance and speed.

Another difficult ability that humans need to acquire in order to communicate with each other is understanding their languages and learning to speak. I have learned that human children take about three years to master one language, and they do so naturally and with ease. In my present situation, while attempting to communicate with several humans from around the world, I am currently learning to understand many languages at once. There is quite a range of sounds that humans can make and I have been enjoying listening in various parts of the world to the many utterances, notes, clickings and gurglings they emit throughout their day, while realizing how peoples and nations speak in so many varied tongues. The story of the Tower of Babel appears to be true, after all! There does not seem to be a universal language in which all people could be able to communicate; no wonder they have such trouble understanding each other! I thought I would at first concentrate on learning the most popular language that the greatest number of people employ, but I soon found out that even within this one language, which is called Chinese, there are many dialects and that their pictorial alphabet consists of thousands of hieroglyphs or symbols. Thus I switched to a different language which seems to be somewhat easier to learn, which is the language of their advanced technology and is called English after part of a small island called Britain. This island is inhabited by a race of people who, over centuries, seemed to have traveled far and wide around the world, spreading their culture, ideas and vocabulary, as well as their policies, their legal system and imperialist designs.

Ah, but I must also mention that some of their music and some of the notes they are able to produce either by singing or by using their many diverse musical instruments are quite divine and clearly inspired by thoughts of God and all those permanent values that we uphold and love so much. This rich heritage of theirs, however, has to be found in amongst the many cacophonies and sound abominations that they perpetrate upon their own and everyone else's ears as well as the sensitive receptors of those angels or entities that are prepared to listen in the hope that the human race has at last produced something meaningful and inspired.

Continuing in research mode,

Hark

the trainee angel

Week twelve

Dear Gabriel

I have made further progress in my attempt to fulfill my next tasking. If you remember, this was to witness a meaningful conversation on Earth where the subject of life after death would be introduced and would have a more lasting effect upon the life of at least one of the interlocutors. As you know, recently I have been researching humans and observing how restricted they are by their need to live and breathe within the confines of a physical body. I have been noting down my reflections to do with my wonderment at the human's ability to live in a carcass, seemingly with ease and few ill effects. Just to watch them feels very strange and heavy and slow and I cannot understand how they can learn to master, for example, walking with such ease and to navigate their way through life, hardly using their ability of astral flight or thought travel.

Anyway, I found a likely candidate for my research in the person of a young student who was on holiday from college and traveling across country to visit his girlfriend. I was watching this boy standing on the side of the road and waving down passing vehicles with his thumb sticking out, pointing towards the direction of the traffic. This meant that he was requesting by gesticulation for a car to stop and give him a lift. When I realized this, I helped him by using a little bit of my powers of persuasion to get the driver of an oncoming vehicle to stop and offer him a ride. Sure enough, the car I had concentrated on stopped and the driver, a man in his forties, asked the boy where he was going.

"Ahead," he said with as much confidence as he could muster.

"Get in," the driver said and I noted that the younger a human is, the less ceremony seems to be applied by a so-called adult responder. "I'm only going as far as Main Street," he added, as the boy closed the car door. "But you can have a lift to the station."

"That's fine," the boy said, pleased to have a ride. He responded to the driver's inquisitive look before the latter had a chance to ask the question, "I'm on holiday. Just wandering around. What about you?" He wondered whether he was sounding too bold for his young years.

"Oh," the driver said, almost dismissively. "I'm off to a meeting. Very boring," he added, after a brief moment of silence, as if trying to look at his commitments through the eyes of the young, carefree boy.

"So why are you going?" the boy asked with a note of genuine surprise and miscomprehension.

"Because I have to."

"What do you mean, you have to?" Still no comprehension.

"It's part of my job. If I don't go, I'll get fired. If I get fired, I don't get paid. If I don't get paid, who will pay the bills?"

"Don't you enjoy what you do?"

"Enjoy? What is there to enjoy?"

"Well, was it always like that?"

"I don't remember. I don't think so. Things have

changed lately. I have more responsibility these days."

"Are you married?"

"Yes."

"Children?"

"Two. Two girls."

"You sound as if they are a burden."

"Oh no, the girls are lovely. Six and eight. Full of energy. They grow so quickly. And I just don't seem to get the time…"

"Make the time."

"Easy for you to say. You don't know what it's like. But, just wait a few years, you'll see."

"I am in no hurry. I've got lots of time."

"Wait till you're my age. Then you'll see."

"Why? How old are you?"

"Forty-five in February."

"Well, you're not dead yet. You could live for another forty years or even more. It does happen. Imagine that! You might be only halfway there. You don't want to waste the next 40 years, do you?"

"Certainly not!"

"On the other hand, you could be gone tomorrow. You just never know."

"How come you're talking like this at your age? You must still think you are immortal."

"I am immortal." The boy laughed as he tossed his head back.

"Well, there you go. I thought so"

At this point I do have to admit that I interjected subtly and influenced the conversation, though I could only do so because both men were open and relaxed, and the young boy was especially prone to convey my promptings to the older man.

"Maybe you're immortal, too," the young man said. "There's one thing I do know. And that is that you have to find the time to do what you want to do. Like spending time with your wife and kids. Otherwise they'll grow up and you'll be strangers to each other. After all, money isn't everything."

"It's all right for you to talk. Your parents probably take care of everything for you. Just wait a few years. You'll change your mind."

"No, I won't. No, I won't. I'll just think of you and I'll remember to remember."

"Remember what?"

"That there are more important things in life than making money. That you should fulfill your natural talents and discover what you are here for."

"Why? Do believe in life after death?"

"Believe? I know!"

"You're a strange boy. How can you know about life after death at your age?"

"I just know."

"Anyway, I park here, so you've got to get out now. Thanks for the company."

"Thanks for the ride. Think about what I said. I think there was a reason for your stopping to pick me up today. I don't know what made me talk like that; I hope it wasn't offensive. I never talk like that to older people. It must have been something you needed to hear."

"Perhaps you're right. Here's my card. If you need anything, call me at the office."

The boy took the card and looked at it. "John Peters, Attorney at Law," it said. "So, I got myself an attorney," he thought. And at the same time I had unexpectedly fulfilled one of my taskings, because as the man drove away, with my angelic powers that were active at the time, I could see he was thinking about the strange encounter and about the possibility of life after death.

So that is it for now. More news next time.

With renewed hope,

Hark

the trainee angel

Week thirteen

Dear Gabriel

I am still learning about human limitations of being in a body. If only they knew the freedom of traveling at the speeds we are accustomed to, although you have assured me that humans can do so with their minds, rather than their entire beings. I remember you teaching us at Angel Academy that a human can stay in one place all their life, but mentally travel throughout the world and the universe, providing they have trained their faculties to do so. I also remember you saying that as the human race has been losing its ability to mental travel and its memory of how to do it, it has found an ever increasing need to physically travel in order to compensate for this loss. This has then resulted in the need for faster and faster modes of transportation, culminating in the appearance in the 20th century of airplanes, rockets and fast boats, trains and cars.

Scientists insist that nothing travels faster than light, and yet their minds can. When they think about a faraway planet or a faraway country—they are there in an instant. When they think of the past or the future—they can time travel as well. And yet, they say this is not travel, this is the imagination recreating images in the brain, which have nothing to do with external reality. How can I convince them that this is not so? I can hear you saying, "Don't.

It's not your job. Stick to your taskings and let the other, more experienced angels deal with the greater and more difficult tasks." But I cannot help it that I am growing up and beginning to see more and more as I progress.

But back to being in a body and the fact that a body causes the human to need a home for shelter from the elements. I have noticed how humans who live in buildings need windows to look out of so that they can observe the world from the safety of their homes. Windows also let the light into their shelters, so that they can see better during the day.

As mentioned before, I have also learned to appreciate how legs must be a very cumbersome means of transport and although they do work, they are very slow and monotonous, offering no respite from the continuous "left, right, left, right, left, right" rhythm being drummed out against a pavement or a floor. And this leads me to another observation—everything seems hard and unyielding here and even their shoes must be mostly uncomfortable and constraining. I have also discovered that, due to this resistance, some humans have found a way to treat their feet to softness and freedom. Every once in a while they take these appendages of theirs on a trip to the seaside where they can enjoy the softness of the sand, the fluidity of the water and the freedom of being barefoot for the day. They probably would not see it that way, thinking that they make the decision to have a holiday because of a need for a rest, but I have noticed that they are greatly influenced by their feet, as well as their stomachs and various other parts of their anatomy. When something ails them, as it tends to do, because on the whole they do not treat their bodies very well, all their thought processes rush to the part that is in pain. They then look for a quick fix and try to solve the problem with a pill or potion. They seldom consider the cause and try to find out what went wrong in the first place. In ancient times medicine took a more holistic approach to illness and disease, but in these fast moving times, people no longer seem to have the patience to wait for the body to correct itself, with the help of natural herbs and remedies.

As you have taught us, we, the angels, guardians and unseen entities, can help heal and make well, but only if the humans we are trying to support take the time to give the body the respite and chance to repair it needs to perform its curative miracles.

In healing mode,

Hark
the trainee angel

Week fourteen

Dear Gabriel

Human eyes appear small to me and it must be like looking through two keyholes, always to the front of their faces. No wonder the human view of everything is so limited! When making a return journey down a road or a country lane, they always make two journeys, not one. One is coming and the other is going and each offers totally different views and discoveries. But they don't seem to understand this and assume that a view seen from the west is the same as a view seen from the east.

Humans tend to think in black and white, always subject to the great Law of Apparent Duality—everything for them is either right or wrong, good or bad, fine or coarse. No wonder they get so upset when they continuously discover that the world is not quite what they had expected it to be and that it will not conform to their invented rules! They do understand that the planet has two expressions—night and day, but somehow they haven't drawn the further conclusion that they can only experience one of these at a time, or be caught in between the two which they call dawn and dusk, whereas the planet experiences both all the time. If they took this line of thought further, they would appreciate that a planetary view offers a greater understanding of duality and that in order to liberate themselves from their parochial comprehensions they need to house the two sides of everything. This would allow them to rise above a single-sided argument into the neutral position of mental arbitrator or angel, adopting the greater planetary view which is unbiased and the only view that counts in universal terms, which we know so well.

In my next letter I shall communicate more news from the fascinating experience of observing human behavior. I am so glad I really am an angel and am looking forward to the time away from time when, defying gravity, I can fly with you again.

In promotion of human development,

Hark

the trainee angel

Week fifteen

Dear Gabriel

You forgot to tell me (or should I say, "warn me") about food! I have never seen anybody eat physical substances before! How strange that humans can do this and not become ill! They put the weirdest things and combinations of things into their mouths and their faithful digestive tracts proceed to extract from them what the body needs to survive. When they are hungry they feel strange sensations in their stomachs and then, as they pass by their kitchen, where food is prepared, or if they are outside and walk by a restaurant or a food store (both are places where food can be obtained for money) and smell the scent of food, they suddenly realize—it is time to eat! Hunger is simply their internal workings letting them know that they are ready to receive. It makes me think that of the four foods known to man—solids, liquids, air and impressions—we angels are very lucky to only need the fourth and finest to live on—electrical impressions or stimulants.

So here I am, realizing the preoccupation humans have for these digestible substances of theirs and beginning to understand why they spend so much time acquiring, preparing and eating them! Of all the foods, the coarsest seems to take up the most of their time, which appears to me to be the wrong way around. So I've learned another lesson—a human needs food and without it they get desperate and although they can survive a very long time without physical nutrition, they seem to need it psychologically more than physically. So much so that they tend to eat even before they are hungry, for their actions are governed more by the clock than by the real requirements of their bodies. And while many people don't have enough to eat and go hungry, others take the time to do all kinds of things with their food—they color it, flavor it, pump it up with gas, irradiate it, add things to it, heat it, freeze it, wrap it, package it, cook it, grill it, bake it, fry it, boil it, broil it, steam it, cure it, smoke it and recently they have even begun to genetically alter it! They add things to things and give the resulting concoctions new names and then claim to have invented something new. They then teach others how to prepare these inventions of theirs and thereby become experts at food preparation and presentation. Other humans seem to specialize in telling people what to eat; many such specialists write books and at any given time you can read conflicting opinions on the subject presented by various authors representing so-called dietary schools of thought. Cook-books are among the best-selling writings here on Earth, while literature concerning how to think or how to live is not nearly so abundant and certainly not to be found on the bookshelves of most humans.

The whole process of buying, preparing and eating food has been blown up to such proportions and levels of importance that it takes up far more time than the thinking about and preparation of the other three foods which are indispensable to the human, namely water (or liquids), air and electrical impressions. Humans here seem to live such a mirror glass existence; everything is upside-down and inside-out. If only they could get their priorities straight and concentrate on what is really important; if only they would learn how to think properly and to take in energizing impressions, rather than ones that debilitate and weaken, then perhaps their eating habits would automatically improve, for they would instinctively and clairvoyantly know what is good for them and what is harmful to their systems. They could go into a supermarket, run their hand over the vegetable counter and instantly pick out by the tingling in their palm which ingredients they were short of, and which were necessary to ingest for the benefit of their ongoing health. They would also know if the water they were drinking was too hard, too soft, too rich in iron or carbon or any other ingredient. Furthermore, they would know where to take themselves to find the water or air with the proper ingredients they needed at the time. Thus they might end up spending different times of the year in different parts of the country, or indeed different parts of the world and perhaps the old-fashioned expression of "taking the waters" or "taking the air" would become fashionable again. However, so much of their water and air is polluted with chemicals they themselves have manufactured and distributed into the environment that there are not many places left on Earth where taking the water or the air can still have as healing an effect as it used to.

Continuing my research into the great eating and human behavior.

Yours in essence,

Hark

the trainee angel

Week sixteen

Dear Gabriel

It feels as if I have been here a long time—that elusive, earthly commodity that is so under-rated here on this planet that people even try to kill it, as if they could! They also give it and take it, as if it were a Christmas present; they make it (though I have never seen the factory where they have the audacity to do such a thing), or lose it and find it (though I have never seen it stashed away in a railway Lost Property Department). They even say they can buy time, but no one mentions selling it, so I don't know how this purchase is being made…

They use other curious expressions to do with time, like having it on their hands, though I have never seen it there, or spending it, though I have never observed it being accepted as a currency in one of their commercial establishments.

Time is a strange word, for it also signifies the process of multiplication. Thus three times four is twelve, or two times six is also twelve. Perhaps this is because time multiplies things and gives the human an allowance and opportunity to fulfill his or her plans. As a person lives, they are given the permission to give themselves away, thus leaving behind a trace of time spent and memories created which can then be reconnected to by all those who follow thereafter.

Time is measured in seconds, minutes, hours, days, weeks, months, years, centuries, millennia, eons, eras—on an ever increasing scale. Each of these units of time can be subdivided into minor units; thus, even a millennium has a definite and finite number of seconds (I have, in fact, calculated the exact number, but it would take up too much space to try and quote it here). A second is a curious word because it also means that it follows the first, and when something appears in time, it has had to have had a life elsewhere first. For example, for a child to be born there needs to be the necessary pre-conditions for it to appear on Earth—a sperm and an ovum need to come together in the miraculous occurrence that humans call conception. The same word applies to the coming together of a thought process, which can then precipitate the arising and birth of another thought, an action, a piece of art or a plan. Thus within a second something new can be born, a destiny can change and a first actually happen, providing there is a coming together of the right conditions for the emergence of something new!

In research mode,

Hark

the trainee angel

Week seventeen

Dear Gabriel

I have been researching other periods and eras which humans relegate to the realms of history and I have discovered that there have been times in the planet's story when people worked together, fought for freedom and what they believed in, helped each other and adhered to tribal loyalty. There have been heroes and saviors and great statesmen, leaders, poets, prophets and philosophers. If a world war broke out tomorrow, or if there was another plague, humans would no doubt again discover new heroes and leaders. The question I am currently pondering is, how can we help people come together in times of relative peace, when the difficulties facing the human race are even more dangerous than those encountered during the plague years? For in the plague years the enemy was visible and common and known to all; today the enemy lies in insidious attitudes, lack of value, non-thinking and deadly assumption, not to mention greed, possessiveness, laziness and "don't care."

I know there are good people on planet Earth; the first difficulty is in finding them, motivating them and bringing them together, then in helping them develop a view that is larger than personal and encompasses not only their own needs, their neighbor's needs, but the needs of the ecology, the planet and the future. It is clear to me that you were right and that this job is too big for a little angel like me. However, I will continue to try and make a small chink in their armor, so that when the big guys, or should I say, the important angelic personages come to do their work, already some groundwork will have been laid.

In continuance and at your service,

Hark

the trainee angel

Week eighteen

Dear Gabriel

This place never ceases to amaze me. There are so many people and more keep arriving every day. How on Earth (literally) am I supposed to get round to everyone? More to the point, how on Earth (literally) do people expect to be able to feed and look after the young if so many new ones keep arriving? I have been told (by your good self) that the human is the most intelligent organic life form on Earth, and yet they seem so very short-sighted… Most of the time I wonder what do they actually do with those sophisticated brains they have been given.

But back to my task. Even if I concentrate on a small area on Earth, the numbers of people living there keep fluctuating. These humans have become very nomadic in the last hundred years and they are always changing places. In fact, many of them (at least in the so-called developed world) seem to travel so much that they no longer feel patriotic about a place—a country, a village, a town, a city or community; instead most often they have become patriotic about themselves. It is no longer as it was in your days when you could look after a community in one particular village and expect few changes over the course of a generation (gene-ration?), except perhaps a few births, a few deaths and very few new arrivals from outside. Although throughout history there have been great migrations, wars, movements of people, invasions and Crusades, these were times when people traveled together for a purpose, in a way that was predictable and planned. Today there seems to be no rhyme or reason to these peregrinations (you always taught me that an angel should use learned and old-fashioned words, to help preserve the richness of the human language and to authenticate our communications when they do occur because ever since biblical times archaic language is expected of us) and diasporas, though the discrimination and bigotry that originally caused the first migrations still prevails. However, these days it is more hidden and masquerades as progress and emancipation.

On the positive side, there is a new phenomenon that has occurred in the last few years—people seem to believe in us more and more, though it is mostly their romanticized ideas of angels that they believe in. They write books about us, paint our pictures, reproduce the artwork of the Old Masters, make little effigies of us and decorate their homes with us (as well as their stationery and their wrapping paper). You should see the stores at Christmas time—there are so many figures of angels everywhere that you cannot escape them wherever you go. Angels sell! (But sex still sells more.) And the funniest thing of all is that each religion seems to claim us for their own. You especially, dear Gabriel, are known and respected far and wide and your good works (or at least some of them) are well-known and remembered the world over.

This makes my job both difficult and easy. Difficult because somehow I need to break through people's pre-conceived notions about the angelic Host if I want to be able to establish any kind of communication between humans and myself; and easy because many do believe that we are out there, ready to help and assist a human who is open enough to embrace the idea of transformation and refinement, or is simply prepared to look at life, if only for a moment, from a non-materialistic point of view. If only people realized that everything physical is far less real than the unseen worlds, that all they can touch, measure and sell is only the end result of an unseen cause, spark or initiative! The material end result of an inspiration, such as a painting, sculpture or writing, will decay with time, but the spark that caused it will remain indestructible forever, ready to inspire another person who is open enough to receive it.

One little angel can only do so much and I do keep trying, but sometimes I get so frustrated with the humans' backward way of thinking, I almost feel like giving up; but, as you say, "don't give up—forgive down"!

Yours reflectively,

Hark

the trainee angel

Week nineteen

Dear Gabriel

Good news, good news! I have found a friend. A human friend. Oh, how everything has changed for me. This little girl is only six but she senses my presence and she talks to me. She can only do so when her parents are not around, for they keep telling her that I do not exist. So we wait until she gets tucked in by her mother at night and then, when she hears the footsteps fade away down the hall, she starts speaking to me, very softly. At first I did not answer, but now that I feel confident that she really believes in us, I have begun to respond. I have not shown myself to her but I have addressed her using our telepathic method and she receives my voice in her head. Her mother tells her that it is just her imagination that she is hearing, but both she and I know that our conversations are real.

And so I tell her things, things I think she can understand with her young perception and young experience. For example, I have told her why she should look after herself and why it is important to wash, brush her teeth, comb her hair and eat the meals her mother prepares for her. Unfortunately, although her parents do encourage her to do so as well, they never explain why. I try to tell her about the future and how she will need to be strong and resilient in the years to come. I tell her that important changes are coming to this planet and that she needs to be ready to face them together with others of her generation. I have also told her that each human is born on to Earth for a reason and that it is a big part of their tasking to find out what that might be and to develop their natural talents to become useful both to themselves and the world around them.

I also tell her a little bit about our worlds. This is much more difficult because no one in her environment—neither her parents nor her kindergarten teachers, nor even her friends—acknowledges that these "unseen" worlds are real. Yet she senses their existence and instinctively knows about auras, atmospheres and lines of force radiating from the planet and from her eyes, fingers and chest. Every time she enters the classroom she sits down in a place that feels safe and comfortable to her—her choice entirely governed by her sensitivity to the frequencies and unseen potencies that surround her. I tell her that what she feels is real and that the heat she senses when someone is angry, for example, is real as well. This is our secret and perhaps this little girl, if she perseveres and further develops her sensitivity, can become a teacher or a healer when she grows up, as all humans were given the choice and opportunity to do.

With renewed hope,

Hark

the trainee angel

Week twenty

Dear Gabriel

I must tell you something funny. When I first started to hear everyone's prayers and requests, I wondered who Money was and thought that this must be a very powerful and benevolent leader, and that he (or she) was loved so much that people wanted him (or her) to be multiplied, increased, looked after, protected and added to. I went on search of this great personage and when I realized that he lived in many great palaces and other smaller buildings that can be found on almost every street corner and are called banks, I thought that this must be a very powerful magnate indeed. Imagine my surprise on discovering that "money" is only a token of exchange made from dead trees and planetary metal! People here seem very attached to these bits of paper and metal, mostly with heads on them, and more recently to numbers that are recorded on a computer screen in "their" bank. Curiously, they devote more thinking time to this than they do to their own health, wellbeing and future, not to mention God, our Lord and the universe!

There is a saying here among humans that "You can't take it with you" and yet they behave as if they can, investing their time in physical things, in the appearance of their physical bodies and in the amassing of wealth. There are those few who care not for worldly possessions and put their time and effort into helping others and attempting to refine the place they live in, be it their home, their community or their country. I have found a few selfless ones who by their actions and sentiment are growing a special substance that can survive their physical departure. If only they realized that there are others of their kind and that they are not alone, perhaps then their efforts would not be assumed to be in vain. For I see that the destruction of this planet has gone far enough and unless some individuals find a way to put a stop to the many levels of pollution that take place here, I really cannot see how the human race can survive beyond the next century.

Please send some help. The human race needs us— it needs guidance and instruction. Ignorance now is greater than ever before, for it is disguised by a wealth of information, far too much for anyone to properly assimilate or understand. Somehow we need to help people rise above their greed, bigotry and ignorance to a new level of being. The human race needs to go back to the classroom, to see how temporary their physical world really is. A building is a man-made construction that begins to wither the moment it is built. Fame might last a generation or two, but who remembers the so-called stars of yesterday? Even their greatest works of so-called "art" will eventually return to the earth and turn to dust. But the process that caused them will not. Imprints within our realms of force remain and either are of a quality that can accompany a person on their journey towards the light or will keep them arrested and Earth-bound (or moon-bound) forever.

I know you know this, for you have explained the ways things work on planet Earth many times before, to me and all the trainee angels, as we graduated from the Angel Academy. In a way, I am reminding myself so that in dealing with humans I do not forget how real the unseen worlds are and how lasting electrical imprints can be, especially if they are motivated by the holy substances of care, compassion and service. May I have the strength to transmit this importance to those humans who are open to receive, so that they may progress into their awaiting lives, where there can be no continuance without these universally required life-sustaining ingredients.

In diligence,

Hark

the trainee angel

Week twenty-one

Dear Gabriel

There is a curious phenomenon amongst humans. On the one hand there is a growing sensitivity towards the natural worlds, with people exploring new ways, which are really very old ways, of healing and attempting to live in harmony with nature. On the other hand the big industries are becoming more and more unnatural, with greater and greater reserves of toxic substances and the increasing uses of radioactive materials. It is almost as if there is a race between the two tendencies and no one knows who will win—will the planet be polluted beyond repair or will the humans mend their ways in time to preserve life and their own future? Already it seems that this planet has survived and outlived all estimated levels of pollution possible; the question is how much longer can this go on, without a dramatic change occurring? I remember you telling us that this planet is heading for major upheaval and change and people here know that there have been many predictions and prophecies warning that life as they have known it is about to end and that the planet will soon enter a completely new stage of its evolution.

There are those who see this coming, and yet even as they voice their fears and their warnings, I wonder how much they believe their own words and whether their vision is great enough to be able to expand beyond what is known into new territories and perceptions. When I see that someone is on the right path and open to the truth, I try to help by encouraging them to think differently and by opening up their visionary conjectures; however, this work is slow and difficult. I have adopted several individuals who are bold enough to think differently and who are sensitive to the needs of the ecology and the subtle balances and harmonies amongst all life on Earth. These are people who do not tend to get carried away by their emotions and sense of righteousness, both of which can make even good people as closed to the truth as those who lack their sensitivity or vision. I try to give these humans the strength to continue in their quest for truth and reality, for, as you have told us, this planet can only survive if enough people believe it can and are prepared to think beyond their personal interest, recognizing their integral connection to the environment they live in. Although there are those who can see the existing trends affecting the future of the planet, they are still the precious few; in my study of human psychology I have come to realize that mostly humans act when it is too late and rarely heed the voice of true reason.

If only humans knew how fragile the life of their great inventions is and how there will come a time when they will discover a far greater power than their so-called electricity and re-discover a new (to them) kind of current that does not require generators, wires and transformers, but can be used naturally any time, anywhere, without toxic side-effects, as applied by the early Egyptians. This planet is so full of undiscovered wonders and riches that I marvel at its beauty and its potential. But those who have the potential to create the greatest beauty of all, the beauty of a conscious mind, seem to be forever asleep.

I do hope I do not fall asleep as well during my stay here. It is an ever-present danger, just as you warned me. In order to remember to remember I continue to repeat to myself those wise and comforting words that you gave me before my descent to Earth:

> "By birth you belong
> To the realm that was created
> Before the emission of time,
> When all was one.
> There you shall return
> When your work is done."

With continuing vigilance,

Hark

the trainee angel

Week twenty-two

Dear Gabriel

I feel a little bit more confident about this place and its inhabitants, in that I now know my way around this beautiful blue ball humans call Earth. I have seen its lands and seas and although it seemed vast and varied at the beginning of my stay here, to the point where I mostly did not know where I was going, I have now covered most areas, flying from the North to the South Pole, following the air route established by that planetary messenger and symbol of endurance, the arctic tern. When researching east and west at varying altitudes, I discovered I did not have to fly anywhere at all, but simply released my attachment to the Earth's gravitational field and waited for the planet to rotate, as she followed her natural course, rotating on her own axis. That way I travel at a thousand miles an hour in human terms, without moving at all!

Thus now I know where is east and where is west, though I do not understand how humans could determine which is which on an ever rotating, ever changing sphere. I've seen the oceans and the lands, the mountains and the valleys and I have watched the little people of the planet, called animals by humans, struggle to eke out an existence for themselves in their ever-shrinking habitats.

Sometimes I manage to communicate with humans and for a moment they stop what they are doing and listen to me, briefly perceiving their own life as part of a larger living system, for once understanding the need for the protection of the environment. But then they tend to forget as they go back to their habitual ways of going on. And those who do listen and remember, sometimes become so obsessed with their newly acquired singular mission that again they lose sight of the whole fabric within which the environment is the weft and human life is the warp, concentrating, as they tend to do, on one issue, like saving the whale or preserving the rain forest or banning the bomb.

And so, what I see my job to be is to help people think differently—less of themselves and more of others, their environment and the world they live in. It is to help them try and grasp a greater view that does not end at their doorstep but stretches beyond this planet and this life even into eternity.

It appears that there are those who are open and who listen. Only yesterday I spent a few moments with a young couple who stood above a cliff looking down at the Grand Canyon. Despite the other tourists around them, for a short moment they were overcome with awe and they understood, albeit briefly, the immense power of the planet; they felt a wonder inspired by her magnificence and magnitude. This new sensation made them feel very small, but not in an insecure or powerless way, for they felt at one with powers and forces so much greater than their own. They knew at that moment that it was the grace of the ordering of the natural world that allowed them to continue to live and they felt grateful and at peace with one another, with the forces of nature and with themselves, wondering what unleashed powers lay dormant within them, for they sensed that inside was an undiscovered continent waiting for its Marco Polo of the mind.

As they turned away and walked hand in hand toward their car in silence, I accompanied them and felt that here perhaps were a couple of the "new people" that you had told me to look out for on my travels around the world.

As if in confirmation of this discovery, I also began to notice that several humans around this globe of theirs have attempted to detach themselves from the destructive trends of the culture by living in various isolated parts of the world, relying on their environment for those basic human needs—food, water, warmth and shelter. They have been harnessing the powers of the sun, the wind and the flowing water to cater to their everyday needs. However, they do find it difficult to escape their upbringing and so they tend to take their culture with them in their minds and it forever affects the way they think. I see that here is a challenge that perhaps I can rise to, by promoting new ideas influenced by the laws of the real world and the needs of the future.

Undaunted,

Hark

the trainee angel

Week twenty-three

Dear Gabriel

Today I answered a human prayer. You have told us not to interfere in the lives of humans and to only respond when we are requested, petitioned and sought after. I remember your caution well and I have always heeded it, stepping back at the last moment, waiting for the human bipeds to ask, before attempting any kind of communication with them or putting into practice a rescue mission.

Today I actually answered a prayer and saved a life, or rather two lives. Remember the couple I mentioned in my last letter? The ones who felt a unique and rich connection to the planet they live on, having visited the Grand Canyon in what humans call North America? They were driving along a windy road, quite fast, when suddenly and unexpectedly they hit a wet patch. The car skidded and turned sideways to the direction in which they had been driving. The man instinctively slammed the brakes with his foot which, of course, made things worse and the car started skidding faster towards the edge of the road and a 20 foot drop below. The woman started screaming, "Save us, save us," so I felt I had the right to intervene and just as the front wheels were about to hit the edge of the cliff, I stopped the car with a jolt. They realized there was no logical explanation for the car to stop there and then and as they were pushed into their seats by the inertia after the car had come to a halt, unscathed, they just sat there for a moment, stunned and unable to speak, wondering what had just happened to them. I then did one more thing, just to teach them a lesson and to show them that they had been helped and that the woman's request had been answered. I just jolted the car very slightly, so that it moved another two inches towards the precipice and then again I caused it to come to a stop. The man and the woman looked at each other incredulously and although nothing was said, they both understood, for silently they each independently said a little prayer of thanks for their rescue. Very slowly the man, with a shaking hand put the car in reverse gear and inched his way away from the edge. Carefully he straightened the car out and they drove away, feeling a little closer to the idea of their own mortality and to the value of the short spark they call life.

Nudging forward,

Hark
the trainee angel

Week twenty-four

Dear Gabriel

I enjoyed performing today's task. All I had to do was find those humans who had completed an assignment they had set themselves and were actually satisfied with the results. There weren't that many to be found, but there were a few scattered all over the globe. There was a child who had finished a drawing of his house, which was his homework for school, and he was taking a good look at it, tongue pushed forward, protruding from his mouth, head cocked to one side. He liked the drawing very much; it was the best he had ever done.

Then there was the book-keeper whose figures tallied up after he had closed the cash register and was working out the bank deposit for the next day. There was the investor whose stocks had gone up; the farmer whose crop was unusually abundant; the writer who sold his script to a movie company and the cook whose meal was praised by the restaurant clientele.

To all these people I managed to convey the message that although they had done exceptionally well and in fact there was really no one in the district who could compete with them, they could still do better, and do it for something bigger than themselves and their own local need. I tried to let them know that everything they do in this life is preparation and learning, so they should not expect perfection from themselves. On the other hand, there is always room for improvement. Perhaps next time they will have reason to be even more pleased...

And so, true to my own advice, I will try to do better next time, too.

Persistently,

Hark

the trainee angel

Week twenty-five

Dear Gabriel

There is this curious law on planet Earth that is called the law of entropy. The word is derived from Greek and means "turning toward." It says that the moment something is made or created, it starts to deteriorate or moves towards becoming equal to its environment (as in the example of ice melting in a glass of water). This is true for any material creation by humans, but not true as far as anything divinely created and alive is concerned. There does, however, come a moment in every life, whether fauna, flora or human, when it turns from growing, becoming better, stronger and more resistant to diseases or demise, towards deterioration, ending in inevitable death or destruction.

In the human case the turning point is 11 years old—it is at this stage that statistically a young person is more likely to die with each passing year. Of course this figure is artificially low because young humans (especially the men) often put themselves in the way of danger and die young unnecessarily. Also, there are many places in the world where the lack of sanitation and proper hygiene, or poverty, draught and illnesses bring about premature death. If the humans could live a natural, healthy life, that figure would most probably be closer to 25. But after that, aging begins and within a few years a person might notice that their energy levels "are not what they used to be."

So aging is accepted as a part of living, even though it is often struggled against and delayed by all possible means—physical, chemical or psychological. I wonder what life would be like if people grew younger with each passing day. They would still have to settle to the fact that they would end up unable to walk, talk or speak, as they would end up experiencing being a baby and becoming dependent on others for all their needs.

The result of these deliberations of mine is a knowing that the only way to really live is to "seize the day" and value the present moment, where all is possible.

With value for the now,

Hark
the trainee angel

Week twenty-six

Dear Gabriel

There was an old, old lady sitting on a bench in a park. She was old in Earth terms, that is, not in ours. After all, you were working your hardest on Earth five thousand years ago and continued to do so for over three thousand years, so that three major religions acknowledge and revere you. No one ever considered you to be old then and even now, no one here would consider you old. But humans these days do not live long at all, so 70 is definitely considered old, 88 is seen to be an unusual achievement and anyone older than that is assumed, rightly or wrongly, to be senile, demented and is mostly treated like a child.

So there she was, definitely old in human terms, definitely "past it," obviously with time on her hands, as she was sitting there rather aimlessly, watching the world go by on an unusually warm, sunny September afternoon. If you remember, this is the time of year when the days and nights are almost equal in length and when in the northern hemisphere, where most people in the world live, summer is coming to a close, the harvest has been gathered and the children are back at school. There is a mellow sense around, as the year is drawing to the end of its third quarter, almost spent, but with gently warm weather and pleasant breezes bringing with it the scents of fall flowers and herbs.

So, sitting on the bench in the park she was reminiscing, calling up pictures, faces and stories from her life, as older people often do. She was once very beautiful—in human terms, that is. I must explain to you a little bit about what beauty means to the human race, for it has nothing to do with our understanding of beauty at all. To them someone is beautiful if they are pleasing to look at and it only applies to young humans, who have not yet had the marks of character etched upon their faces. Thus it is "skin deep" and demonstrates their passion for the unformed—perhaps because they enjoy having power over others and prefer to look at a youthful face that in their minds they can mold to their own imaginary screenplays or scenarios.

So she had once had such a face, beautiful in human terms, but now it was lined and wrinkled, marked with experience and years—much more beautiful in our terms! As she sat there, a young couple walked by, hand in hand, enjoying each other's company and the balmy gentleness of the early autumn breeze. She remembered what that felt like, being out on a date—the newness, excitement and promise of it all. I could feel her remorse and regrets that never again such an experience would happen to her and I decided to help her have a better appreciation of who and what she was. I switched the two women around so that the younger one was now sitting on the bench, looking out onto the world with older eyes, while the older one was walking hand in hand with a young man, her body firm and young again and her eyesight clear and sharp. Both women thought it was a dream or a vision, as it lasted for only a few seconds, but due to the experience they both received an understanding that they would have never come to on their own.

The old woman was young again and although she now had exactly what she thought she wanted, she was also overwhelmed by many conflicting emotions, feelings, desires and dilemmas that young age can bring. She no longer knew who she was or what she was good at, for she had yet to discover her still hidden talents, abilities and skills. She now lacked the security of knowing her way around in the world and she could feel the many yearnings and urges that her young body and mind were promoting: there was so much she wanted to do, so many places she desired to see. She could feel a youthful ambition gripping her every cell and flooding her body with an overpowering energy, which she had no idea how to contain. She felt like doing many things at once and at the same time realized that she would need to go through many experiences and thousands of days like this before she would be able to settle with confidence to the knowledge of who she thought she was. She wondered about the man whose hand she was holding onto and realized that she was not secure in this relationship; it needed more time to prove itself and she did not yet know whether it was something she really wanted or not.

At the same time the girl on the bench, having found herself in an old body, was looking out at the world with wonder and understanding and she felt an odd relief from the many pulls, pushes and urges that she had been experiencing only a moment before. Her whole body relaxed as she leaned against the back of the bench and simply enjoyed being there in the moment—something she had never felt in that way before. There was nowhere to rush to, there was nothing to do, arrange or organize; there was simply her and the world around her and the fact that she could now be part of it without the fear, doubts or driving ambitions that had plagued her since her early teenage years.

As mentioned before, it lasted only a few seconds and then I switched them back and they both were relieved and glad that it had only been a fleeting moment and that they really were who they thought they were. Both gained from the experience—the older woman emerged from it more settled to the fact of old age creeping up upon her and the younger woman was pleased to once again feel the return rush of energy that kept her going. She had also won for herself a recognition that old age had something to offer too and the beginnings of an appreciation that as she would go through her days, months and years, she would have the opportunity to win a wisdom and settlement that could bring her peace and reconciliation in her old age. She gently squeezed her boyfriend's hand, glad that he was not a figment of her imagination after all. Although nothing was said, she walked on more contented than ever before, valuing the moment and no longer expecting or hoping that it would last forever.

So, another task has been completed and I, too, have gained some wisdom from the experience of the phenomenon of human aging and although I still do not fully understand its meaning and purpose, I am beginning to appreciate that every stage of a life's journey is an opportunity to live in harmony with nature's plan.

I remain yours in continuing training,

Hark

the trainee angel

Week twenty-seven

Dear Gabriel

With the experience since my last letter, I am finding it harder to handle the feelings in me, which can be summed up by—"I want to go home; I've had enough!" I know you have warned me about the mid-tasking crisis and I think this must be it. When you told us that we would find Earth, or rather human dealings on Earth, difficult, inhospitable, off-putting, repugnant, you were talking about the Earth of 2000 years ago! It seems to be very different now from your descriptions and much worse. Humans no longer trust each other, respect each other or behave decently towards each other. Greed, suspicion and ambition rule the day.

Technology has entered people's lives in unprecedented ways. They no longer converse or make music together or share their stories; they prefer to watch moving pictures on the box they call a television set or on a large screen in houses specially built for this purpose. Those who can entertain or make others laugh or convincingly can cause a story to appear as reality inside their boxes and from their screens are the most highly rated humans on this planet and everyone knows their names and likes to read about them in their newspapers and magazines. Those who can find ways for their technological boxes they call computers to perform more tasks quicker and better are those who are the most powerful and richest men (and women, though technology is mostly a domain dominated by men) on Earth.

Humans are so dependent for everything on the earthly power source they call electricity that when it runs out or when the Earth's polarity reverses, as it cyclically does, they will be at a loss as to what to do and how to live. They currently travel great distances in their cars, trains, planes and boats; they speak across the world over their phones and then they watch more moving pictures on their computers and television sets. I don't even know whether they will be capable of holding a decent conversation when they will have to rely on their own wit and ingenuity for entertainment and education.

Some people long for the return of the old ways but it is clear that these could never come back. So, as the planet is poised to change and there is such a need for humans to adjust their behavior and ways, very few people seem open to listen to the voice of an angel.

If only they realized that help is here today, now and that tomorrow could be too late!

In desperation,

Hark

the trainee angel

Letter twenty-eight

Dear Gabriel

As you probably remember, there are locations on Earth that have become portals for universal forces to enter. These are usually places where several ley lines converge to form a nexus, or hub. Some have been there for centuries, like Stonehenge on Salisbury Plain in Wiltshire, England, or the site of the pyramids in Egypt or Mexico, while others form up briefly to allow a higher power to enter and then dissipate. Still others move around to appear first in one place and then to reappear where next needed. Through these gateways we, angels and other unseen entities, try to communicate with humans in various ways, transmitting high energies, healing force and creative inspiration.

I have been shown the latest attempts to communicate with the human race that have been instigated by intelligent beings from beyond this galaxy—they have been configuring designs and diagrams in fields of wheat and other grains and grasses. These signs and symbols are called crop circles by humans, because the first ones of these were indeed in the form of circles, but these days they appear in many different geometrical shapes, including triangles, waves, and straight lines. Humans are still puzzling over these diagrams and are finding it difficult to interpret the messages contained therein;

what I am trying to help them understand is that there is intelligent life in the universe beyond planet Earth, and that there is attempted help coming from the unseen worlds. In fact, as we know so well, the universe is a unity of purpose, and the human belongs to this great enterprise and has a part to play, by right and by heritage. I am desperately trying to help the human realize this and act with a dignity that reflects their divine origins.

In pursuit of excellence,

Hark

the trainee angel

Week twenty-nine

Dear Gabriel

There is something strange going on with the little people, which people call animals, here. Humans lock up the creatures of the planet in small cages and sell them from what they call pet shops, or they bring various species together in large cages and call it a zoo (which is short for zoological garden—I did my research!), so that other humans can come along and show their children different varieties of animals.

I spoke to the little people in the small and large cages and they have a completely different view of the situation; they see that humans are behind bars and they also see that the humans watching them are not free. Humans cannot do as they please and even though they have no chains or handcuffs, they are constricted by many things: by their own laws which increase in number and become more complicated every year as another loophole is discovered and blocked; by the laws of the planet which they would wish to defy and attempt to do so with many new clever inventions; by their own engineering which they tend to push beyond its limits, not realizing that it is limitless in its possibilities, but not in the way they had thought; by their own emotions which attach themselves with a suction action to other people, to things and to places in ways that make it difficult to help them become released; and by their false sense of security which makes them very afraid of change or anything new.

They do talk and sing a lot about freedom, but their ideas of what this means are so antiquated, that they still use the word to refer to liberation from the times of slavery and serfdom when one human being would have the power of life and death over another. This makes them feel superior, for they firmly believe that they have moved away from tyranny and bigotry, not realizing that these two are very much alive and well, but have moved underground or rather inside, and tend to reappear in much more subtle ways. So I think the little people have a better idea of what real freedom means, so I will be consulting with them concerning the idea of living a natural life.

In pursuit of the truth,

Hark

the trainee angel

Letter thirty

Dear Gabriel

Humans seem to crave power and they continuously insist on comparing themselves to others, not realizing that every one of them is totally different and unique and would require a completely individual measuring device to assess their progress. They like to carve out for themselves a niche, a success, a win, so that they can feel satisfied that they are doing well. But doing well by what criteria and by whose standards? Mostly by their own evaluation, based upon their understanding of wealth and power, which is measured and seen almost exclusively in material terms only.

It is so rare these days for me to be able to find someone who is interested in real wealth, the kind that exudes out of a person's eyes with warmth and encouragement, that passes from human to human in their offering of a healing touch, a piece of unbiased advice or a token of real care. I see it sometimes as it is extended from parents to their children, within families and among friends. Yet it is a rare commodity and often destroyed before it can be learned and translated into an internal glow, whereby a person would be able to offer it from self to self, becoming the steward and custodian of their own marvelous machinery, offering it healing, care, consideration and true and just government.

I am trying to help humans see that they should listen more often to their own internal sensings, reactions and sensitivities. If they could understand that the best clock or measuring device is inside them, perhaps they would not have this continuous need for watches and alarm clocks. Do you know that they have invented machines to measure their blood pressure, to listen to their heartbeat, to see into their bones, to measure the level of their body heat (which they call temperature), the electrical activity in their brains and to find the many ingredients in their blood or urine? They ignore the evidence of their own feelings and sensings, often overriding the many signs given them by their own bodies, and relying with greater confidence on these many inventions of theirs. They take pills to quell symptoms but seldom deal with real causes or question why they are being attacked by a disease. Instead, they get themselves examined by specialists and rarely take the whole organism into consideration.

Freedom of the mind is something I am currently trying to impart to those I manage to communicate with, giving them a sense of the richness and complexity of their own beings.

With self-renewed hope,

Hark
the trainee angel

Letter thirty-one

Dear Gabriel

Something unexpected happened today. I was sitting on a branch of a tree in a park in a place called Australia, contemplating the many taskings that still remain to be done, when a woman walking by spotted me. Of course I was not really sitting on a branch, as I have no body parts with which to sit, but it could have looked as if I was because I have taken to the habit of imitating humans so that I may understand them better and thus learn how to help them, or rather, how to help them help themselves. Now this woman was walking underneath the tree, which was a large chestnut in full bloom with white scented flowers, when she unexpectedly stopped and looked up, straight at me. It was quite a shock to both of us, for I was not expecting her to see me because in my experience mostly humans cannot see angels unless we take on a more physical bodily appearance.

So there she was, looking straight at me, her eyes and mouth wide open and surprise, awe, fright, delight, shock, hesitation, disbelief and wonderment, all appearing on and disappearing from her face in a matter of seconds. Finally, she whispered softly, never taking her eyes off me, "An angel, I really am seeing an angel." I could see she was straining her neck and she was not going to give up or go away, so I descended to a lower branch to avoid injury and so that we could converse more comfortably. Of course, I could have easily simply disappeared, but I felt that her sensitivity should be rewarded, so I followed my instincts and alighted onto a lower bough.

"Yes, an angel, at your service," I said, not with a voice, but with a transmission straight into her head. As she relaxed, I could see the intensity in her eyes and I felt there was something specific she wanted to ask me. I also noted the signs of suffering on her face.

"I feel very privileged to be able to see you," she said quietly and for a moment I thought how strange it would look if anyone happened to walk by and see her talking to what would appear to be a tree.

"I wonder if you can answer one question. I had a little girl, Annie, who was three. She was very sweet and loving and…"

The woman was beginning to cry, her eyes filming over with tears and her voice struggling to articulate the words, but she bravely continued, even though I knew already what she was going to say.

"… and she died six weeks ago quite suddenly. It was a terrible accident." She paused for a moment and looked up at me questioningly. "Why? Why her? She could have brought so much joy and love and laughter into this world." The tears were now rolling down her cheeks and I could see that she had shed many of them already.

I know there are certain things I am not allowed to divulge or pass on, so I thought for a moment and responded to her deeply rooted need by saying, "It's not your fault. There is a reason. In fact, there is a reason for everything, but I am not allowed to tell you what it is. May the knowledge that her life was not in vain be a consolation to you. She has left you with a gift that you can keep forever, as long as you let her go. So, Inez (for that was her name), let her go."

And then I disappeared from view by retaining my radiation so that she could no longer see me, even though I was still there. I watched her for a moment as she stood there, pondering the words I had passed on to her. Then she pulled out a handkerchief, wiped her eyes and slowly walked away.

I felt a good deed had been done and I was pleased to cross out another one of my smaller taskings from the list you gave me.

Honor bright,

Hark

the trainee angel

Letter thirty-two

Dear Gabriel

I am so glad I am not alone in trying to help humans see their real predicament and realistically assess their situation. There are so many unseen friends that help me as I try to help people. So many natural entities, spirits and energies are dedicated to the continuance of this planet that humans call Earth and the further evolutionary trend of the most advanced species that inhabits its surface, that one would think they should have done better over the course of history. But somehow, rather than extend their sensitivities and abilities to see, feel and communicate with their unseen supporters and allies, they seem to have concentrated more and more on the material aspects of things. When you inhabited the Earth and wandered around what is today called the Middle East, nobody doubted your existence or questioned your credentials. They listened and obeyed your messages from the Almighty. And yet, if you were to descend today to the same part of the world, I wonder how long would it be before you started to question the plausibility of your mission here and how long would it be before the very humans you were attempting to help would question your very existence. There are many forces working for peace and towards the securing of a progressive future, but as soon as there is a voice of reasonability and pacification, there are many more guided by the lower human emotions we have tried so hard to work against: hatred, intolerance, cruelty, vengeance and despair. So many of our best messengers are poisoned, crucified, decapitated, shot or otherwise destroyed by those who are the holders of material power in the world, once they step forward to speak the truth.

There have been many times of uplift in human history, when great men and women would rise above their personal views and opinions to encompass an idea or religious motive. There have been times of great transitions and inspiration, when ordinary people would rise to extraordinary deeds and noble thoughts. Everything here points to the fact that such a time is coming again and many human predictions point to such a revival as well. Again I feel that for us to meet and survive this challenge, we too need to find our common denominator and bring together our energies in the pursuit of the future; we need to consolidate our attempts to educate the human race concerning their natural abilities to communicate and learn from their unseen friends. This time is crucial and we should not miss the upcoming opportunity for helping the human survive further into and beyond the new millennium.

Could you please send me some wisdom or advice concerning this?

In anticipation,

Hark
the trainee angel

Letter thirty-three

Dear Gabriel

As you can imagine, gender issues are new to me. I am trying to comprehend how two complementary halves of the same force unit can develop so much animosity, misunderstanding toward each other and instigate so many power struggles, battles, and so much resentment and distrust.

It is mind-boggling how one half of this human high essence could have subjected the other half with such impunity for so long. And yet, this is the truth—the so-called stronger sex have taken their strength as permission to dominate the so-called weaker sex in a thousand obvious and subtle ways.

The two frequencies—masculine and feminine—are so necessary for the continuance of the many species on Earth and are omnipresent everywhere in nature. I wish that humans would realize that all people are made up of and process both flavors, notwithstanding the gender they are born into. It all depends on who they are and what they do; they each are both masculine and feminine, as far as their energy process is concerned.

A woman performing a masculine paternal act is processing a masculine energy; a man performing a feminine, nurturing act is processing a feminine energy. Neither is right or wrong; both are a part of living. Some men are more feminine; some women are more masculine by nature; the great richness of human diversity is the fact that no two people are the same and that even within one person, the mixture of energies constantly changes and evolves.

Some energies are more easily classified than others. Due to the warp away from what is natural, human behavior, customs and traditions are not easily labeled masculine or feminine in a clear and unambiguous way. A mother looking after a baby is considered a feminine act; a man foraging, hunting and breaking new ground is mostly considered a masculine act. But often the borderline between the two is blurred and unclear: is creativity masculine or feminine? Is compassion masculine or feminine? Is intelligence masculine or feminine?

In the 2000 years since your influence was felt here on Earth, much has changed—more and more activities are no longer defined as strictly masculine or feminine. Life is a mix of frequencies, and what is becoming more defined and clear to those who have the sensitivity apparatus active enough to recognize the relationship between cause and effect is, which frequencies are enhancing to life, to its surroundings and to the planet, and which are polluting and detrimental to their continuance.

With respect for the duality,

Hark
the trainee angel

Letter thirty-four

Dear Gabriel

Recently there have been a number of natural disasters here on planet Earth—storms, earthquakes, tsunamis, tornadoes and cyclones. Wherever disaster strikes, there I rush to help. Not that I can physically repair homes, remove rubble or heal wounds. But there is something I have found I can do, and that is I can influence the mood of the people. Curiously enough, where there is human misery and poverty and disease, as in the aftermath of an earthquake or a storm, there is also the opportunity for high feelings to gather, such as compassion, care, healing and companionship. People start to help each other in the face of a disaster, and the world rushes its aid and support to areas afflicted by destruction. It is very heartening to observe the dealings between two families who have lost their homes in the aftermath of an earthquake and are in proximity spending the night under the stars in a city park. In such circumstances people who would have never otherwise met, are becoming friends and talking to each other and sharing the last remnants of food that they have managed to rescue from the ruins of their homes.

Regarding the fierce weather conditions that tend to afflict various parts of this blue planet at this time, some humans are at last waking up to the realization that the way they have managed the planet's environment and resources does indeed influence the weather. There are those who claim that this is not so and that weather is subject to cycles or phases of the moon or conditions beyond their control. What they do not seem to understand is that everything is connected and that if you cut down a forest, the micro-climate will inevitably change, the soil will erode and the winds will become stronger and more destructive.

The relationship between human activities and the weather had been known about in ancient times. And even today, among the indigenous tribes of North America and Africa there are those who know how to cause the rain to fall, by performing a ritual and invoking the elements. It works every time and yet there are those who do not believe this is so.

I have also noted that the weather has a major influence upon human behavior and moods. When the sun is shining, everyone is happier; if it is cloudy for long periods of time, people become sad and depression can take hold in a community. It is a known fact that in countries that have fewer hours of sunlight during their winter months, there is a higher rate of clinical depression and more suicides are recorded each year.

However, it works both ways and people can influence the weather, just as the weather can influence them. I was watching a group of schoolchildren today as they sat on a bench in the school playground during their lunch break. They were looking at the sky and I could see the silent concentration on their faces. Curious, I flew over them to see what they were up to and then I realized that they were collectively attempting to disperse the clouds overhead. And do you know, it worked? By their efforts (with a little bit of help from a friendly angel) the clouds rolled away and made enough room for the sun to shine through for the remaining time of their break. As soon as the sun shone through, they started laughing, got up from the bench and started playing with a ball they had brought with them. It was a joy to see their satisfaction and sheer enjoyment of the moment!

In experimental mode,

Hark

the trainee angel

Letter thirty-five

Dear Gabriel

As you have taught to us, everywhere in the universe life is sacred and the commandment "Thou shalt not to kill" is upheld (theoretically at least) in all religions, all traditions and all legal systems. However, as you have warned us, and I was surprised to witness, there are places and times on Earth when killing is not only permitted, but downright encouraged. I am of course referring to wars, which humans seem to wage continuously—there always seems to be some war going on somewhere on this blue planet of theirs, and very often sanctioned killing goes on beyond the battlefield and is an unfortunate result of acts of aggression or dominance implemented by one nation or tribe upon another.

So although most people on Earth adhere (theoretically) to the commandment "Thou shalt not kill"), most would agree that there are circumstances when breaking it is permissible. I do not see how they can accept such a contradiction, unless it is in the name of self-defense or preserving life other than one's own.

Upholding the law,

Hark,
the trainee angel

Letter thirty-six

Dear Gabriel

Just a brief note today. I have engaged in a new discipline so that I may remember to remember my mission here. I have noticed that without constant fortification, my resolve can easily weaken. Yesterday I became frightened when for a brief moment I could no longer remember why I was here. It is so easy to become lulled by the constant repetition of one day following the next, by the regularity of the sun and the planets and the stars. It was only a very short moment, but as I looked around, I knew I needed to remind myself constantly that I am here to help the progression of the human towards their next evolutionary step, as long as they want to be helped.

So, to keep a long explanation short, I have added to and deepened my morning and evening dedications so that I can remember my task and my sacred duty. Having done so, I realized that I had followed the already well-trodden paths of generations of humans who have established this very same discipline for themselves and have called it their morning and evening prayers. The difficulty begins when even prayers become routine and meaningless. Thus I have decided to now call my prayers remembrances and make sure that every day they are new.

There is a habit among some humans to say a prayer of thanks giving before they eat; they call it grace. And indeed humans are graced with an abundance of foods, flavors and variety that adorn their tables. Many times these prayers become routine and mechanical and lose their meaning; but when said with feeling and genuine appreciation for the gifts that they receive, these human prayers find their way, in the form of a wave of energy, beyond the sphere of the planet, out into the darkness of the universe where they can enhance another life, another civilization or even another planet.

I know that what I am doing here can also help beings in other places and at other times facing similar struggles. Thus I need to be true to myself and remember the many gifts I have received as well. Perhaps I do not ingest physical food, but for the wisdom and teachings of my elders I am truly thankful.

In dedication,

Hark

the trainee angel

Letter thirty-seven

Dear Gabriel

It seems like a very long time since I have last written to you, and since I have heard from you, though in planetary terms only a week has gone by. (I am still learning to adapt to the earthly concept of time.) This is not because I have forgotten or adopted some of the lesser ways of the human to which you have given the names avoidance, laziness and procrastination. No, I am well aware of my duties and obligations to you and your superiors. But I am also painfully aware of the fact that you are absent from me, for I no longer feel your presence. I worry that you have abandoned me and I wonder why. Perhaps I have been here too long and am too much involved with human, planetary and mortal frequencies and thus it is no longer possible for you to communicate with me or for my messages to reach you. Perhaps I am now too coarse to have dealings with an archangel of your magnitude and perhaps you will relegate my reports to some lesser angel. Perhaps I have not been performing here to your satisfaction and my results are slow to manifest. Perhaps you are waiting for my next attempts and consequent results before you send me a reply. In my brighter moments I also think that perhaps you are giving me a free hand to take the next initiative on my own, without advice or recommendation from you.

Whatever it is, I have no intention of resting, giving up or waiting idly until my next instructions arrive. There is much to do and I will not cease until I see some results in the world around me.

So, today I flew over a town and as I did so, my only and intensively singular thought was to radiate peace and harmony. And do you know, I think it did make a difference. As I looked into the homes of people through the roofs and walls of the buildings, I saw families get together and friends spending time with more care and interest in each other's needs and with a greater desire for sharing than otherwise would have been possible. Old grudges became forgotten and even some television sets that are always on were switched into their darkened mode to make way for conversation and exchange.

It was very satisfying to be able to make a difference in this way and I am certain that once experienced, such a moment will be repeated by those who were part of its arising, this time perhaps with a conscious decision to make it so. And although human memories tend to be short and not very efficient, maybe today's experience will have left a more permanent mark. Thank you for your patience with me and for allowing me to determine my own course of action this day.

In progression,

Hark
the trainee angel

Letter thirty-eight

Dear Gabriel

As you explained to us in the Angel Academy, the clues are everywhere for those who have eyes to see. Take, for example, color. You do not need to taste a plant, or smell a flower, or touch a fruit to receive the first indications as to its energetic properties. Color is the first transmitter, because it is received by the eyes, before the other senses have a chance to participate in the experiment.

So, for example, a red tomato will have different nutrients and healing properties than an orange carrot or yellow squash. People sometimes ask why there are so few blue foods on planet Earth, and I have to laugh, because no one as yet seems to have made the connection that as this is a blue planet, there is little need for blue foods, because blue energy is everywhere in abundance.

There are indications that some humans are realizing the significance of color and the fact that different energies are surrounded by different colors, wearing them like a cloak. Some people are beginning to recommend that people should eat foods of many varied colors. There are also people who can see color in other people's auras, and around plants and trees, and are beginning to recognize how these radiations change as a person becomes, for example, afraid, angry, delighted or impatient. Each emotion has its own color and people are drawn to the colors that are compatible with what is already inside their aura; thus what a person wears tells a story about their current feelings and moods.

Energy appears before the manifestation of matter and influences the physical shape that houses it. Thus the smell, facial tensions, posture and movement of a person tell so much about who they are and what they think about. Each body behaves, moves and adjusts according to the soul and spirit that reside inside; if a different spirit were to occupy the same body, everything about the outward manifestation of that person's thoughts, behavior and feelings would change as well.

Thank you to all our teachers at the Angel Academy who tirelessly taught us about the five expressions of energy, registered by the five human senses (touch, hearing, smell, taste and sight), which can then be decoded by the human brain (providing the human has learned to use this precious and very sophisticated cosmic instrument).

With gratitude,

Hark

the trainee angel

Letter thirty-nine

Dear Gabriel

Today I influenced a human and helped him after he had crashed his car into a tree. It felt so difficult to witness this accident, for as I watched, I sincerely wished I could have helped, but on this occasion I knew I had to wait and be patient, and be there as a comforting presence after the fact. I also knew that without this incident this person would have no value for life, no respect for his own existence and no acknowledgment of his own fragility and transience. This arrogant soul, full of success and self satisfaction, would have been lost forever if not jolted into a new recognition of the meaning of life and what its consequences might spell out for him. It hurt me more than it hurt him to see the accident happen, but a broken wrist and a few facial scars is such a small price to pay for the acquisition of a new chance at salvation or of recognition of one's own mortality. He had been drinking—not a lot, but enough to not notice a spilt pool of oil on the road until it was too late—and the car skidded off the tarmac onto a grassy verge and into a tree. Dazed, he sat there for a while, with pieces of glass lodged in his face, bleeding and with a sharp pain in his wrist—a result of pressing his hands firmly against the steering wheel to break the impact of the car hitting the tree.

Another car came along and he was soon taken to the local hospital where his face was cleaned and his wrist bone set. It was clear that his injuries were only temporary and that he would heal quickly, leaving very small scars on his forehead and jaw. The moment that made the difference was just before the impact when he thought he was going to die as he saw the tree rushing towards him and when he suddenly realized how much he loved his life and his family and all the things that he had yet to do on this Earth.

He is now recuperating and thinking about his own mortality, about life after death, about God and about his purposes as a life on planet Earth. He is trying to find new ways to show the people he cares about that they are dear to him; he is taking his time to think about his future, his dealings and his aims. He has decided to give up drinking and he is even a bit more careful about what he says, how he formulates his thoughts and with whom he spends his time. He is also thinking about how he treats his family and his staff at work and he has decided that he must show them more appreciation and gratitude for their support and the work they are doing.

So, although this was a painful incident to witness, I do think the good results outweigh the danger involved, which, of course, does not mean that from now on I will be going around looking for accidents all over the place. For I understand that I must evolve too and always find new ways to do good in this world.

Pressing on,

Hark

the trainee angel

Letter forty

Dear Gabriel

Here on Earth people, animals and everything living are born comparatively (compared to an adult specimen, that is) small. They then grow to full capacity—usually mainly in height, but also somewhat in breadth and width. The internal organs develop as well, until the moment comes when growth ceases and deterioration sets in. In the human terms this is called aging and scientists have been looking for the reasons for this process and the exact location of the aging gene.

There are stories and traditions about humans living for hundreds of years—much longer than they live today. Everyone wants to live longer—they think this life is better than the next. It makes me laugh, because when a person clinically dies and is then revived, they have what is called here a near death experience. When this happens, the process of crossing over begins and sometimes they are met by their deceased loved ones and family members and are invited to proceed into the light. They feel immense joy, relief and happiness and unless they have serious commitments and unfinished business on Earth (like, for example, the duty to bring up children or the need to pass on a message to humankind about their experiences "on the other side"), they usually do not want to come back. If they do return to this life, they then know for sure that there is indeed life after death and that life here, with its worries, pain and aging, is nothing compared to the joy of passing on to the next life.

I try and help people envisage their next life and am currently involved in comforting the elders of the human tribe—those who are becoming ill and infirm with age. I have come to realize that aging really doesn't need to be like that—it could be a lot healthier process and more enjoyable for many people, if they had made better choices throughout their life, leading up to old age. We all pay in the end for the decisions we make!

Facing reality,

Hark

the trainee angel

Letter forty-one

Dear Gabriel

Today I was asked a curious question (the question was directed into the ether, rather than to me personally, but I managed to intercept it). A woman was walking down the street in a small town in California in what humans call North America, when suddenly, for no apparent reason, a picture flashed into her mind. She suddenly saw herself standing on a subway platform in New York; she had lived in Brooklyn when she was younger and used to travel every weekday to Manhattan to work by subway. The question she wondered about was why should she think of a place she had not visited for years, for no apparent reason. I popped an answer into her head, so that she would have something new to think about. I told her (telepathically, of course) that perhaps someone in New York standing on that very same subway platform was thinking of her. Sometimes when people think of a place or another person, they are simply picking up another person's thought process. We know well that when someone thinks of another person, a lance of energy travels to that person, wherever they may be, and if they are open and awake at that moment, they might just pick it up. That is why, often when people phone their friend or relative, they might be surprised to hear the other person say, "I was just thinking about you."

I do know there are questions we are not supposed to answer, like when a parent asks why their child who has not yet lived a full life, has been diagnosed with cancer or some other terminal disease. In fact, adults often ask the same question about their own predicament leading with the question, "Why me?" In response to that one, I remain silent, because I know they will find out the answer in the end (or when the end comes) and that it is not for me to explain the reason why. After all, there still need to be (and always will be) some mysteries that cannot be explained within this earthly dimension, but will become clear in the next stage of a person's journey.

With discretion,

Hark

the trainee angel

Letter forty-two

Dear Gabriel

One of my greatest current concerns is to do with the environment here and how to protect it. Everywhere I look the human hand has added, taken away, relocated, excavated, used and abused the natural resources. I see that there are individuals who try to preserve, protect, conserve and clean up the ecology they find themselves in, using whatever means at their disposal, but they are still very much in the minority. In fact, the destroyers and abusers by majority own the land, the resources and the power, whereas those who wish to protect the environment mainly work by dedication, determination, a pioneering spirit and with value for the planet they live on. To give you an example, I must tell you about one specific act of heroism: there was a woman in California who spent two years living in a giant 1000-year-old redwood tree, to save it from logging. There are also those who have taken upon themselves the defense of the whales—they go out onto whaling grounds in their boats and disrupt the hunters' illegal efforts to kill. As I write this, I can hear you say, "Admirable, but one redwood tree or a few whales will not save the planet."

I have reluctantly come to agree with you that neither of the mentioned stances is going to educate the human race to mend their destructive ways, because collectively people will not do anything seriously about the environment or their own continuance until their very existence is threatened and survival becomes their number one priority. At this time they think they still have time and in their usual short-sighted manner they procrastinate, delay, put off and turn a blind eye to what is really happening all around them.

Thus I see my function to be to cause a realization here, a glimpse of the truth there and above all, a real concern for the future. If I can help humans come to realize that their children will be affected by their actions and that life as they know it cannot survive yet another generation without taking a very heavy toll on their well-being, security, prosperity and health, then I will consider that my tasking has been well fulfilled. However, the real issue I am facing is how many concerned individuals will it take to tip the balance in favor of survival. For I see that there are those who care and there are those who live for the moment, for profit or are simply too ignorant to see the real situation and the impending inevitable changes that will surely wreak havoc upon their misguided lifestyles. So in the meantime I satisfy myself with slighting housewives' hands to add less detergent to their laundry or influencing them to choose a more environmentally friendly washing up liquid! I do look forward to the day when I can participate or even be influential in global changes, when the new human will be able to see clearly the effects of his wrongdoing and mend his ways.

Thus, I continue in earnest,

Hark
the trainee angel

Week forty-three

Dear Gabriel

I still find it difficult to acclimatize myself to the fact that time on planet Earth appears to be linear. Humans seem quite settled to this phenomenon and have come to expect that each day, as they get up in the morning, they are one day older and that each day they mark another date off their calendar. It does account for predictability and constancy in their lives—they have worked out the movements and progression of the stars, the sun and other planets in the solar system in relation to their own plans and forecasts. They see the sun rise in the east and set in the west and according to these observations, they have ascribed qualities to each of the four directions of the compass. Perhaps this predictability is why they find it is so difficult to accommodate change and aging, especially if it happens fast or surprises them early.

I sometimes wonder how they would fare in our dimension where the past, the present and the future are all part of a three-fold appearance and where the contemplation of any event, phenomenon or chain of events has three manifestations: its history, already completed and thus fixed, written and unchangeable; its present, where there is malleability, flexibility and susceptibility to alteration and change; and its future, where millions of possible strands lead in every direction, visibly indicating possible outcomes and progressions. They can understand this concept when playing with a pack of cards, in a game they call "bridge," for example, where there is only a limited number of possibilities as to which cards are held in the hands of their opponents. Each of the four suits has 13 cards and each of the four players is dealt 13 cards from the complete deck; thus the person on a player's left or right can only have in their hand at the beginning of the game at most 13 of any of the four suits minus whatever number of cards the player holds in his or her hands and minus those which are revealed on the table. (If you do not understand the rules of this strange game of theirs, it is simpler to consider a lottery where a person needs to choose, say, seven numbers out of the total possibility of 49). But when it comes to considering the future, the possibilities are limitless and humans seem unable to mentally embrace all eventualities. Thus they end up concentrating on only a few possible outcomes which inevitably causes them to become disappointed and to claim (with some degree of accuracy) that the future is unpredictable. They never seem to be able to take into account all possible ingredients that make up the unfolding of coming events, as there is always something they had not been able to foresee. Their brains, after all, are not fully evolved yet and they are only able to handle a limited amount of information at a time.

Perhaps this is why they are so short-sighted and unable to see very clearly beyond this year or next. This strong myopia of theirs causes all kinds of errors and bad planning, as if they can't quite believe that the future is already being written by what they do and think in their now. Another example of their inability to successfully predict the future is their difficulty in recognizing the evidence all around them and foreseeing that they themselves in their turn will age and wither as all their seniors had done before them. Everyone else grows old, so why can't they see that they will as well?

There are many other examples. The whole fuss about their computers not being programmed to handle the changeover at the end of the twentieth century because they had been set up to respond to only the last two digits of a four digit date just confirms this short-sighted flaw of theirs. It manifests itself in all that they do, for very few prepare themselves for their next life while living this brief earthly existence of theirs. They spend a lot of time debating the possibility of life after death, but when it comes to living the truth of what this might portend, they seem to ignore the evidence of their own learned writings, the advice of the sages and the many belief systems which have given them clear indications through the ages as to what awaits them after the demise of the physical body.

They have ignored the teachings of many with more experience than I, so I do not expect the majority of them to listen to me. But perhaps, by giving a few of them a brief insight into the future, I can turn the tide of the destiny or fate of a precious few. I do so want them to realize that they hold the keys to their own future and that although while on planet Earth they cannot reverse the insistent onslaught of time, they can master its implications by making decisions as to who they want to become and what they want to do in this life as well as the next one.

There is a saying here on planet Earth that "Seeing is believing" and I often wonder, if the unseen became seen, how would that alter human behavior? If they could see the energy they manufacture by their thoughts and deeds, if they could measure the strength of the radiation of their emotions and desires, would they be more careful as to what they allowed themselves to think about and to feel?

Working for small successes,

Hark

the trainee angel

Week forty-four

Dear Gabriel

I remember from our Bible classes, how you used to appear to people to predict important events or to tell them what to do. Full of good tidings and prophecies, the angelic tasking used to be to herald the future and be a harbinger of news. There are also more recent stories in which illuminated winged figures seem to have appeared in order to change the course of a battle or to warn of a particular oncoming event.

Today there are no angels with household names, but the old, ascended entities, such as yourself, are still remembered, quoted, respected and prayed to. Thus some people think that you are still around, awaiting their summons and willing to respond to their demands. Their prayers, however, have changed their character from those you used to quote to us in the Angel Academy. These days people seem to be more interested in amassing material possessions and in their quest for power than in their need to be saved.

I absolutely refuse to respond to requests for things, jobs, positions, money, to settle affairs of the heart or the need to dominate over others or manipulate situations to a person's advantage. As you have advised us, I wait for the genuine cry of the lost, searching for real understanding, wisdom and the truth. And if and when

I hear such a call, I respond as immediately as I can by divulging a small item of knowledge or an insight to help the person on their way. The rest they have to do themselves, to find the source of learning that will lead them towards the treasury of views which is waiting to be opened by those who care and want to know. I help a person step outside of their personal preoccupation with self into a much greater picture where they are no longer the center of their own universe. Sometimes this can happen in a dream, sometimes in a moment of clarity, but throughout this experience I remain anonymous and watch their reaction from the sidelines. Sometimes such an effort is quickly forgotten, misunderstood or ignored. But sometimes it works and awakens something deep inside the person so that they can begin to look at life for what it is, governed by the laws of the universe and subject to those principles, which have been established here from the beginning of time. When this happens, I see there is a hope for the person and that they have possibly embarked upon a journey of self-discovery and search for truth. Still rare, these moments have been recurring and I am glad to say that there are those who are beginning to question the reason for their existence and are beginning to look beyond the surface level of superficial and temporary truths.

So therefore I am in pursuit of the permanency of all things which has taken me into the following directions: into the minute worlds where constancy rules and where an atom of carbon remains an atom of carbon and where even the unstable elements consist of indestructible sub-atomic particles which have remained the same for millennia. And further still, into the worlds of electricity and magnetism, which, although changing their form all the time, remain immortal. Energy cannot be destroyed and therefore its function must be divine. I have also been researching and attempting to connect to the large worlds which we know so well—those of stars and galaxies and universal inhabitants which although shifting, moving, evolving, being born and dying all the time, are nevertheless a signpost to permanency and reliability. These are my anchors of sanity where I can see the godly laws of nature and the creation reflected and fulfilled.

When I become concerned about the ever-changing focus of the human attention, I can always return in my contemplations and meditations to these truths and realities that enrich my life and have always caused a security and inspiration.

Consistently,

Hark

the trainee angel

Week forty-five

Dear Gabriel

In my continuing training as an angel, I have been contemplating the meaning of the word "service." I know this is part of the angel training curriculum and that there is a need for me to embody this quality if I am ever to be a more useful angelic force.

So, being that I am currently resident on planet Earth, I have looked at the human usage of this word. I saw that people are being served, for example, in restaurants, stores and other establishments when they require something or some action to be performed for their benefit. The "service industry" is based on the sale of services, rather than material goods, whereby humans can have other people, who specialize in various fields, do things for them, like cut their hair, wash their clothes, repair their cars, clean their carpets etc.

And then I noticed people going to church on Sunday for a "service." This was interesting because during the service their religious needs are being catered to by another person, in this instance a priest, vicar or deacon. He (more often than not) conducts the whole ceremony, including the intoning of prayers, the giving of blessings and communion, which is supposed to be a direct connection to God. He also delivers a lesson for the day, which he calls a sermon. The idea of this short talk is to shift people's attention from earthly matters to thoughts of God and the Host; however, the person delivering the sermon is not always successful in doing so.

They have funny jokes here on Earth and they do love to play with words. I overheard one man saying to another, "I took my car in for a service, but it wouldn't fit in between the pews." This caused some hilarity and laughter from both of them.

The requirement upon me is to be in service to you, to the Host, the mission and the Almighty. I am in training to have the very essence of service radiate from me to all those I come into contact with. It seems to me that this ability should become an integral part of my dedication and the purpose of my existence. Clearly one can only truly be in service when one has at least some understanding of what one is in service to. This is perhaps why service is an advanced requirement within the Angel Academy curriculum and does not appear on the list of compulsory assimilations for the lower levels of angel trainees.

Always there is something to be in service to, unless, of course, one is the Almighty Himself/Herself. Though service must live with Him/Her as well, for isn't He/She the very embodiment of service? I do not presume to rise above my station to even try to understand the function of the Almighty One; therefore will I continue these deliberations from my own level. I see my entire existence, my raison d'être (as the French speaking people refer to it), to be in service to all who wish to refine and promote good, compassion, improvement and Samaritan behavior towards themselves and others. Wherever a helping hand is extended or assistance is selflessly offered, there will I be, at least in spirit, offering service.

Perhaps one of the aims of service is to obliterate vice and bring about a unification from deed to deed, from positive attitude to improving attitude and from the strong to the weak who wish to be strong.

If something is regularly serviced, it does not fall into disrepair and is maintained at well functioning levels. If we attend to our reasoning processes and make sure we think, act and do according to our purpose, aims and ideals, then we will never need a superior being like yourself to remind us why we are here. Thus I wish to service my entire being regularly so that I can better serve others and those entities that depend on my work. I also want never to be self-serving, for this is an attitude that does not befit an angel or even a human; certainly not even a trainee.

In continuing learning,

Hark

a trainee angel

Week forty-six

Dear Gabriel

It is very strange, but humans think that God is masculine and always, irrespective of the religion they adhere to, refer to Him/Her as He. This is an indication of the mentality of humans here, forged by years of history, for mostly all of the world's presidents, prime ministers, kings, heads of organizations and other establishments, and most people in power are men. For years now there has been an on-going struggle for women to assert themselves and take their rightful place as equal partners in public life, in social life, in education and in the workplace. However, the men seem to be very reluctant to release their firm grip on most of the resources, the power, the leadership, the land, and all the other riches and desirables that the planet and the human ecology have to offer. This is very strange, because really no one can possess anything. When the human dies they have to leave everything they possess behind, usually bequesting their possessions to their descendants and their close family, relatives or partners. Thus the idea of ownership continues from generation to generation.

I have been working with a few groups of people around the world, whose aim is to establish an equal partnership between men and women. I am trying to help the men realize that with educated and emancipated women by their side, they will become more competent, more intelligent and more powerful, though perhaps not in ways that they understand power to manifest. Perhaps if they could grasp this one simple truth, they would not be so afraid to hold out a helping hand to the women of the world, to bring them into a better position to become the best they can be. At the same time I am trying to help the women understand that they do not need to be in competition with the men, because they bring into the man/woman relationship a unique point of view, a sensitivity and an intuition that the men need to learn from in order to be the best that they can in turn also be.

There still are countries where women are not allowed to own anything and are totally dependent on their husbands, male relatives and family members for sustenance and their daily needs. Sometimes they even have to depend on charity and the generosity of strangers in order to survive. So in my travels I seem to spend more time helping women and trying to lift their spirits and give them some additional hope and will to go on. I do find that women are more open to me and my mission, and they seem to be more spiritually alert. Perhaps this is because the men are so busy preserving their wealth and attempting to increase their positions in the world that they have little time for the messages I send them. Or perhaps, because of their plight and difficulties, the women of the world find solace in long-term visions of the future, thus becoming more forward thinking and more concerned with the hope for a better tomorrow.

There are more women on Earth than men and this statistic seems to have been constant through the years, at least as long as humans have kept records. Curiously enough, more boys are born than girls on a daily basis, but women live longer—they are more resilient, healthier and stronger (not physically, but as far as endurance is concerned). Also, they don't put themselves in so many dangerous situations as men do—men fight wars, jump out of airplanes, recklessly ride motorbikes, wield weapons, drink more and do many risky things with impaired judgment. Some women do these things as well, but not nearly as many die young.

So perhaps the new spiritual revival will arrive through the women. All signs and indications seem to point to the fact that this could be so. Perhaps you could send me some instructions about how to persuade the men to be more open to messages from their unseen friends (including angels, like myself).

In pursuit of real equality between the genders,

Hark

the trainee angel

Week forty-seven

Dear Gabriel

I was watching a young boy in rural America waiting for the school bus early one winter morning. As the bus drove up to the driveway of his house and the boy got on and started greeting his friends, I realized how early a young person is taught about schedules, timing and punctuality. If that boy had been late for the bus, he most probably would not have made it to school, or his parents would have had to drive out of their way to take him there. Everything seems to start at a definite time: school, work, performances, shows, appointments, meetings between friends. Almost everyone in the so-called "developed" nations' Western World has a diary, a schedule, a timetable, a calendar, a clock, a watch, a computer and an alarm clock. They wake up and the first thing they do is check what time it is. When they go to bed, the last thing they look at is a clock. They always know, or are supposed to know, the time, the date and the season.

They also know much more than just the time. News spreads fast and what happens in one part of the world is immediately related to all other parts, with pictures, films and commentary. Perhaps this is why humans no longer need or expect to see angelic messengers—their lives are so ordered, compartmentalized and globally responsive that most events don't seem to make much of an impression any more, just washing by in the general flow and influx of yet more information.

One of the most frequently heard questions on planet Earth is, "What time is it?" And then rush, rush, rush to the next engagement or to fulfill the next deadline. Whatever has happened to time spent between humans, exploring a subject for the joy of discovery, or trying to get to the root of an event or to better understand a human dealing?

I can just imagine an invitation to a gathering saying "Arrive when you feel like it," or "Let's begin when it feels right and there is a sense of unity amongst us." Then maybe, rather than taking a "rain check," which is being open to change due to a circumstance beyond their control (or so they think, because they are not conscious of their own impact upon the weather), they might start taking "mood checks" or "emotion checks" or "people surveillances" instead.

Still puzzling it out,

Hark

the trainee angel

Week forty-eight

Dear Gabriel

Thank you for sending reinforcements—they are so badly needed here. These new angels that have arrived fresh from the Angel Academy are quite playful and optimistic as to the possible outcome of their work here on Earth. It reminds me of how I was when I first arrived and it also makes me feel older and a little bit jaded, even though I have only been here for 11 months. But the work needs to continue as I prepare to leave and there need to be some new, enthusiastic angels to pass on my duties to.

There is a game that these young angels play, after their work has been done and especially if it has been a successful day. They tend to play with the clouds, pushing and pulling them into meaningful shapes and picturesque images. Sometimes a person might look up and see a duck in the sky, or an elephant or a giraffe. The best time for this game of theirs is the evening, when they can add color to their palettes and tinge the clouds in gold or scarlet. Sometimes the whole sky turns rose pink or orange while the sun sets and these angels rejoice as they add tints and hues, perhaps just for a brief moment. Nevertheless, it does brighten the day of many a traveler or local inhabitant, who might just at that moment look up and exclaim, "How beautiful the sky is tonight!" It reconnects people to the beauty of nature and fills them with awe and the inspiration of the moment. It also makes my tasking of working with these angels so much more enjoyable.

So thank you for the companionship and ingenuity of these young angels.

Happily,

Hark

the trainee angel

Week forty-nine

Dear Gabriel

Thank you for letting me know where my next duty will be—one year on planet Zemtylion. As you have taught me before, a year there is not equal to an earthly year, but much longer—more like twenty revolutions of this blue planet around its yellow sun. And each revolution there consists of only fifty-three rotations or days, so the days there are indeed long. The most amazing thing about Zemtylion, that I am trying to understand and prepare myself for, is the fact that in some respects it is completely opposite to life here on Earth. Here there is this strange phenomenon that all humans are used to and take for granted—that it takes a long time to build something, but it can be destroyed in a day or even in a moment. Take the medieval cathedrals of Europe, for example, or an ancient castle or monastery—it might take three generations to complete, but with today's technology, if a bomb were to be dropped upon it, it would be shattered in a moment. Or if natural disaster hit, like a powerful earthquake—it could topple in less than a minute. In recent earthquakes and hurricanes, entire communities were destroyed in a matter of seconds.

There have been times when a special building had been protected by rings of angels, like Cologne cathedral during the Second World War. All the buildings around it were destroyed as the Allies bombed Germany, but the cathedral miraculously survived, unscathed—a site that can be admired and visited to the present day. I wonder if humans realize that we do sometimes interfere in their lives in a positive way—coming to the rescue in a time of need.

But back to the planet Zemtylion—I understand that there it is the other way around—it is very fast to manifest something from nothing, but to destroy it or take it away could take a long time. This I will have to get used to!

I can think of an analogy: here on planet Earth there is a winter sport that people like to occupy themselves with; it is called skiing and a person attaches two long pieces of wood to their feet so they can slide downhill and stay on top of the snow which falls on some parts of the planet, during the cold winter months. They enjoy the speed as they slide downhill, with gravity helping them on their way and accelerating their progress. In their hands they hold two sticks with pointy ends that help push them down faster.

But to climb a hill or mountain takes time and effort, perhaps ten times as long as a slide downhill. So humans have invented ski lifts, cable cars and cog wheel railways to take them uphill without any effort on their part, except the effort of buying a ticket and walking to the departure gate.

So the analogy illustrates how one direction takes effort and time—climbing uphill—while the opposite direction is fast and effortless—skiing down. I wonder if on the planet Zemtylion one would climb fast up the hill and then it would take forever to come down. For this to be the case, there would need to be some sort of anti-gravity at play, pulling upward, rather than pushing down.

Indeed, I don't think a planet like that could survive, as everything would be rushing away from it into space. However, jumping would be easy and so much fun!

In questioning mode,

Hark

the trainee angel

Week fifty

Dear Gabriel

Introducing new angels has been a joy and a real education. They keep asking questions and sometimes I have to struggle to find the answers. They are very inquisitive and willing, eager to get started. They are learning to communicate telepathically with humans and I have reminded them that not everyone is open to listen to advice from angels, whether novice trainees or even fully-fledged guardians. I tell them not to give up and to keep transmitting messages of joy and hope. It is always surprising to me who does listen and who responds; I told them to spend more time with the children who are closer to our worlds and more sensitive to our presence.

It is also remarkable how when one is called upon to teach or lead another, one has to be very thorough and precise; I am learning how best to pass on what I have learned during my stay here on Earth. I am also quickly realizing that any unfortunate habits I may have acquired in the last twelve months can be quickly transmitted as well, and it takes a lot of work to undo a lesson that was taught with errors, to then introduce the correct message in its place.

It is curious how in every school, from time to time there is a year when the number of bright students is unusually high and there seems to be a special grace that enhances the whole group. I feel that this has been such a year and that these angels who have come to Earth straight from the Angel Academy to earn their wings, are going to be very important angels in the future who will be influential in bringing the human race back on track, towards further evolution and a better future.

With hope,

Hark

the trainee angel

Week fifty-one

Dear Gabriel

I have received your message that my sojourn here on Earth is coming to an end. I am very pleased to be transferring to a more elevated galaxy, where the work will be more subtle and more difficult, and perhaps not quite so punishing. I will take with me many lessons from this level of human evolution so that I may remember where these beings have come from and what a long journey they have yet to make. It has been (and still is) quite an education, as I had no idea what level of mental discipline, or rather the lack thereof, could exist alongside a seemingly technologically advanced society. I think part of the problem is that science has run away with its inventions, substituting skill as well as physical and mental agility with gadgets, machinery and computers.

How ironic that the very thing the human has invented to save time and increase production is, at the beginning of the new millennium, now eating up more time than ever and causing more problems than solutions. I am very curious how this situation will be resolved in the long-term and I do wonder how the human will continue to evolve if it relies more and more on external aids and new technological advancements, rather than its own faculties and inventiveness. It almost seems as if the human needs to re-learn how to think all over again, although this time perhaps the result will be more far-reaching than mere survival. It is time for these earthly bipeds to think of their future and the future of this beautiful planet of theirs. Perhaps they have come to a point in their evolutionary journey when they can re-believe in the benevolence of creation and accept the vision of their lives yet to come.

There are so many unresolved issues in the world today—from war to poverty, to pollution and over-population—that I wonder where and how it will all resolve itself in the end. I can only see that the world is hurtling towards global change and wonder how exactly this will come about and when. I wonder if I could be given a leave of absence at some time in the future to revisit the Earth to continue my research concerning the evolution of human life.

So perhaps, after my duties on the planet Zemtylion are completed, I could be assigned to planet Earth for another of their short, yet eventful years?

With hope and curiosity,

Hark
the trainee angel

Week fifty-two

Dear Gabriel

So, this is my last letter to you from planet Earth—a planet I have learned to love for its natural beauty and variety and unpredictability. Many humans who at the present time occupy this domain have many enduring and redeeming features. There are so many of them and although most are driven and governed by greed, gain and loss and the constant need for security and confirmation, there are also those who rise to acts of heroism and selfless generosity, who care for other representatives of their species and protect those less capable inhabitants of planet Earth who in their language are described as members of the flora, fauna and mineral families.

I have performed my tasks to the best of my abilities and I think I have helped further the process of encouraging the human race to awaken to its precarious predicament and need for change. I do regret not being able to see the final outcome of my endeavors and those of my ethereal brothers and sisters, but with the other representatives of the Host continuing the work and with the gradually increasing sensitivity and responsiveness of some cooperating members of the human race, I am confident that the future will be eventually won and that refinement and compassion will reign among these strange two-legged creatures. As stated before, I have observed that although some humans are indeed developing and refining, there are also those who seem to be traveling in the opposite direction—towards further degeneration, despair and depression. I understand that there might be individuals beyond repair who will not be able to make the forthcoming transition and who will not have a future in the new world that is being forged and built upon this planet of theirs. I do regret that there is nothing we can do for them, but I think they know this and even have a saying confirming that angels cannot help those who do not attempt to help themselves (or something similar to that effect).

I enjoyed my time here and I am glad to be going for a second tour of duty to another place in the Great Creation where I can successfully act and be of service, where I can continue to learn more about psychology and attempt to penetrate the defenses set up by still evolving beings in the universe, in order to help them help themselves.

Signing off,

Hark

the trainee angel

www.ingramcontent.com/pod-product-compliance
Lightning Source LLC
LaVergne TN
LVHW011206080426
835508LV00007B/625